This book belongs to

_____

10" PIE
9" PIE
8" PIE

delish

The How-to Cookbook for Young Foodies

Joanna Saltz & the Editors of Delish

.3   4   5   6   7   8   9   10   11   12   13   14   1

Let's Get Cooking!

RECIPE INDEX

Looking for a dish to cook right now? Check out our favorites in this handy list.

I NEVER WENT TO CULINARY SCHOOL.

JOANNA SALTZ EDITORIAL DIRECTOR

Jo,
AGE 8

"My daughter (middle) loves to have fun in the kitchen with her friends. She's not afraid to try new techniques and recipes—even if she messes them up—which I think will make her a better cook when she's older!"

I learned to "cook" the way so many people do—by watching food TV. My favorite cooking shows were *Barefoot Contessa* and *Nigella Bites*. Both featured smart, funny, talented and beautiful women (Ina Garten and Nigella Lawson) who were so relaxed and nice about cooking. "Don't worry if it's not perfect" was their general message, and that attitude (plus the camera close-ups on their techniques) gave me the confidence to try it all myself. I really hope this book will be a similar guidepost for you. The skills in these pages start with the most essential in Level 1 and build up to more complex (and awesome!) techniques in Level 5. You'll find great step-by-step pictures so you can discover the building blocks of cooking, and then you'll get super-delicious recipes to help you put your new skills into action.

But most importantly, the best cooking advice I ever got was from Garten herself, which she wrote in her first cookbook, *The Barefoot Contessa Cookbook*. She said, "I believe a cookbook is just a starting place for cooks... It is very important to give recipes your own style." As you cook from these pages you'll use all your new tools and have fun making all the food—these recipes and everything else you might cook—your own. I know you can do it. **— Jo Saltz**

Grace

Everett

Siri

We all started somewhere.

Our incredible Delish team reveals the best cooking advice they ever got.

Robert, AGE 12

ROBERT SEIXAS SENIOR FOOD DIRECTOR

"**Never be afraid in the kitchen or the food will not come out good.** My grandmother cooked for the Louis–Dreyfus family, one of the richest families in Europe (yes, Julia Louis–Dreyfus's family). She used to make potatoes and Cumberland sausages, roasting both at the same time at an absurdly high heat. I used to watch her when I visited, and the oven/heat made me nervous all the time."

Jill, AGE 3

JILL BAUGHMAN DEPUTY RECIPE EDITOR

"**Read through the entire recipe!** Not just once, but twice, even three times. That way, there will be no surprises, and you'll be totally prepared before making your dish."

Brooke, AGE 3

BROOKE CAISON FOOD EDITOR

"**Clean as you go!** It makes the food a lot easier to enjoy."

Rebecca, AGE 9

REBECCA SIMPSON STEELE VISUAL DIRECTOR

"My granny first taught me to cook. At a young age I learned the important lesson, "Don't burn the flour!!" She was talking about the roux for the sausage gravy and emphasized to **not take your eyes off the stove.**"

Gabby, AGE 4

GABBY ROMERO ASSOCIATE EDITOR

"Whenever a recipe calls for garlic, double it. And **add salt to everything** (even sweets)."

GETTING STARTED

Look Out for These Important Icons

Extra Info: Don't miss these! There's something interesting to know about a skill, recipe, or ingredient.

Test Kitchen Trick: Find out our expert chefs' best cooking secrets.

Master the Technique: The more you know, the better cook you will become. Discover some additional skills.

Caution: Hold up! There's something's hot, sharp, or you might need an adult to help.

KITCHEN RULES

Yes, cooking is fun, but it also requires some attention to detail. While your finished product doesn't need to be perfect, it's really satisfying to have recipes turn out the way you intended. Follow these tips to prepare for your cooking adventure.

1
SET UP FOR SUCCESS

Clear a space on your kitchen counter to become your "station" (just like a restaurant). Wipe down the counter, set up a non-slip cutting board, and wash your hands. Keep your station (and your hands!) tidy as you cook—put away ingredients when you're done measuring them, and wash your hands often, especially after dealing with raw meat or eggs, before serving other people, and before eating.

2
WASH YOUR PRODUCE

To remove dirt, and/or harmful bacteria, it's important to rinse off fruit and vegetables. Hold up on meat though—washing it can actually lead to cross contamination.

3
READ THE RECIPE FIRST

Before you start cooking, read all the way through your recipe. Actually, read it twice! This will be your roadmap for your cooking project, and you want to know ahead of time if there will be any significant curves or roadblocks (like freezing time, long simmers, etc.) so you can plan accordingly. Once you've read the recipe, gather your ingredients and cooking equipment.

4
SEASON, SEASON, SEASON

We often call for specific salt and pepper measurements when it comes to savory dishes because everyone has different taste preferences and dietary restrictions. Season as you go. When your dish is almost finished (and after the meat, if there is any, is cooked), taste it. If it's bland, you probably want to add more salt. Start with a pinch (or $\frac{1}{8}$ teaspoon), stir it in, and give it a try. Then repeat if necessary. Remember, you can always add more, but you can't take any out.

5
ALWAYS ASK AN ADULT FOR HELP...

...when dealing with hot or sharp things. Even if it's something you've done before, it's always a good idea to have a grown-up in the kitchen with you.

6
BE CAREFUL WITH KNIVES

When holding a knife, make sure to keep your fingers away from the blade. Hold the handle with a strong, firm grip. Stabilize the food you're cutting with your other hand, curling your fingertips under so they stay safe. Always use caution when washing, drying, storing, and handling knives and other sharp tools like graters and vegetable peelers.

7
HAVE FUN!

Play around and don't be afraid to mess up. Your food doesn't need to look picture-perfect for it to be downright delicious. And sometimes it takes a few times to get a dish to taste just the way you want it.

MEASURING MATTERS

When measuring liquid ingredients like oils and water, use a liquid measuring cup with a pouring spout. For dry ingredients like sugar and flour, use measuring cups and spoons. Read the markings on your measuring spoons carefully and become familiar with ¼ teaspoon, ½ teaspoon, 1 teaspoon, and 1 tablespoon.

QUICK TIP

If you're ever missing your tablespoon, remember this: 1 tablespoon = 3 teaspoons.

WORKING WITH DRY INGREDIENTS

1
Spoon the dry ingredient into the measuring cup until it's slightly above the edge of the cup.

2
Tap the top of the measuring cup with a spoon to evenly distribute the ingredient inside the cup.

3
Level it off with the handle of the spoon, a knife, or any level tool (don't pack it in!).

1

WORKING WITH WET INGREDIENTS

1
Place the liquid measuring cup with a pouring spout on a level, flat surface.

2
Pour the liquid into the measuring cup.

3
Bend down until your eyes are level with the side of the measuring cup. Look to make sure the liquid is even with your desired measurement.

1

2

3

2

3

SHARPEN YOUR KNIFE SKILLS

Before you start slicing and chopping, it's important to select the right tool for the tasks.

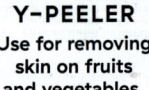

For more about peelers see

P. 33

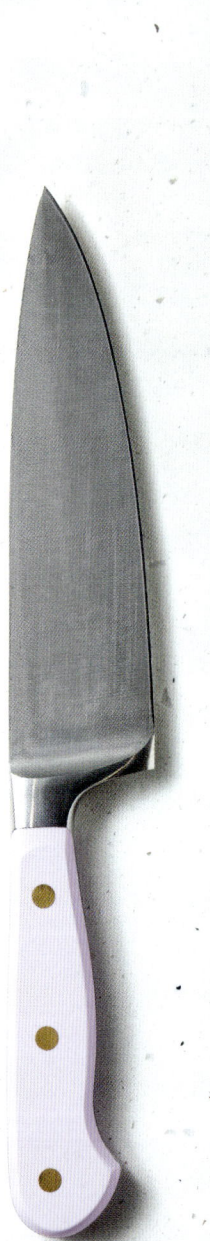

Y-PEELER
Use for removing skin on fruits and vegetables.

KITCHEN SHEARS
Use for breaking down chicken or snipping herbs.

PARING KNIFE
Use for coring fruits and vegetables or making small cuts.

CHEF'S KNIFE
Use for most tasks; it can do it all.

SERRATED KNIFE
Use for slicing crusty bread or tomatoes.

COMMON CUTS

These nine essential techniques will make prepping ingredients for your next recipe a whole lot easier.

BRUNOISE
⅛-inch thick

MINCED
⅛-inch or less pieces

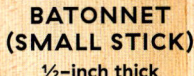

**BATONNET
(SMALL STICK)**
½-inch thick

SMALL DICE
¼-inch pieces

ROUGHLY CHOPPED
¾- to 1-inch pieces

**ALLUMETTE
(MATCHSTICK)**
¼-inch thick

MEDIUM DICE
½-inch pieces

RONDELLE (CIRCLES)
⅛-inch thick

JULIENNE
⅛-inch thick

ROUGHLY CHOPPED
¾-to 1-inch pieces

HALF MOONS
⅛-inch thick

COOKING A TO Z

Important Words to Know.

A

Al dente
An Italian term meaning perfectly cooked pasta: tender but slightly firm. (Not mushy!)

B

Beat
To vigorously stir a mixture, such as whisking eggs with a fork to make scrambled eggs or using a stand mixer or hand mixer to combine the butter and sugar for cookie dough.

Bloom
To heat dry spices with a fat (butter or oil) to make them more flavorful and aromatic. Try this when making Cacio E Pepe. **P. 103**

Boil
To heat a liquid until it bubbles rapidly. You cook pasta in boiling water (which is 212°F). **P. 98**

Broil
To cook food under direct, intense heat. **P. 130**

C

Chop
To cut food into smaller, similarly sized pieces so that everything cooks at the same rate.

Core
To remove seeds and tough centers from fruits (apples, pears) and vegetables (bell peppers).

Cream
To beat together butter and sugar until well combined and lighter in color. It's an important step for a fluffy cake. **P. 142**

Cross contamination
When bacteria from one food is transferred to another object— often from raw meat. This can get you sick, which is why it's extra important to wash your hands and keep kitchen tools clean. **P. 53**

D

Deglaze
To unstick food on a hot pan by pouring liquid into it and scraping the bottom with a wooden spoon.

Divided
When an ingredient amount is followed by "divided," it means that you're using some of the ingredients at different stages of the recipe.

Double boiler
Equipment used to gently cook, or heat food without the risk of burning. To set up a double boiler, nestle a heatproof bowl over a pot of simmering water.

Drizzle
To pour a thin stream of a liquid ingredient (like olive oil, hot sauce, or melted chocolate) back and forth over a dish.

E

Emulsify
To mix together two liquids that usually don't combine easily—like oil and vinegar to make dressing.

F

Fold
To very gently mix ingredients into a batter or dough, usually with a silicone spatula. **P. 168**

G

Grease
To coat a baking sheet or pan with a fat such as butter or nonstick cooking spray to avoid food sticking to the cookware.

H

Hangry
A state of anger caused by hunger. Which is why breakfast is so important! Skipping it can make you extra hangry.

Hors d'oeuvres
The French term to describe appetizers, or small savory bites, typically finger foods.

Icing

A topping (usually a glaze) for desserts commonly made with confectioner's sugar and a liquid such as milk, water, or juice. It's not the same as a frosting, which is usually made with butter and sugar.

Julienne

A fancy way to describe cutting foods into thin strips about 2–3 inches long. Like the carrots in the Cucumber Sushi. **P. 29**

Knead

To work dough ingredients until you form a smooth and pliable mass. Kneading by hand means pressing and folding the dough with the heel of your hand over and over, like in our calzone dough recipe on page 139. It's easy, but it takes some time (and muscle). To make the job easier, you can use the dough hook attachment of a stand mixer. **P. 136**

Kosher salt

We call for this ingredient a lot in this book. Kosher salt has slightly larger crystals than iodized salt (the type that you generally find in a salt shaker). It's also iodine free. (Iodized salt can have an unpleasant taste.)

"Let rest"

It's an instruction we'll tell you after you've cooked meat. Letting your chicken or steak sit for 10 to 15 minutes before slicing will ensure that all the juices don't escape onto your cutting board.

Mince

To cut a food into super-tiny pieces.

Nonstick pan

A skillet with a slippery coating to ensure foods don't stick to it, a.k.a. your secret weapon when frying eggs. **P. 84**

Opaque

When your food is no longer see-through. When shrimp turns from translucent (allowing light to pass through) to an opaque pink—which it will do super fast!—it's cooked.

Oven safe

Kitchen equipment that can be safely used in an oven, such as a cast-iron skillet. (One of our favorite things to cook with.)

Pinch

A small measurement of an ingredient (often salt or spices) that you can hold between your thumb and pointer finger.

Piping

To use a pastry bag or resealable plastic bag (with the corner snipped off) to distribute frosting (such as buttercream) in a controlled and/or decorative way. **P. 180**

Quarter

To cut an ingredient into four equal-size pieces.

R

Reduce

The process of thickening a liquid such as a sauce or stock by boiling or simmering until the liquid has reduced in volume and intensified in flavor.

Roast

A method of cooking using the dry heat of an oven.

S

Sauté
To cook food in a small amount of fat over relatively high heat. **P. 104**

"Season to taste"
To alter the flavor of a dish by tasting and adding more ingredients (most often salt) according to personal preferences.

Simmer
To heat a liquid to just below a boil.

T

Tender
When cooked until tender, a food has become soft enough that it is easily cut with a knife or chewed.

Toss
To combine ingredients gently to avoid damaging or altering their shape, size, or texture.

U

Underbake
To remove a baked good from the oven before it has finished cooking. In cakes and quick breads, underbaking will result in sunken centers and uncooked batter.

V

Vegetarian
A person who does not eat meat and possibly other animal by-products (like broth), often for moral (such as environmental), ethical, religious, health, or dietary reasons.

W

Whip
The process of beating food using a whisk, hand mixer, or stand mixer to incorporate air and increase volume. The most satisfying and delicious example: whipped cream. **P. 174**

Whisk
The process of combining ingredients using a wire whisk or fork. **P. 72**

X

XOXO
The way you might sign a thank-you letter to whomever bought you this book.

Y

Yeast
The scientific definition: a very tiny fungus that turns sugar into alcohol and carbon dioxide, a gas that causes rising. In baking, active dry yeast, instant yeast, and fresh yeast are most common. Each of these will cause baked goods to rise as well as add a distinct flavor and texture.

Z

Zest
To remove the outer rind of a citrus fruit for use. **P. 38**

Taylor-Ann

Charlotte

Robert

USING METRIC MEASUREMENTS

The Delish Test Kitchen develops recipes using standard U.S. measures. Use the charts below to reference approximate conversions.

	U.S.	METRIC
VOLUMES	1 teaspoon	5 mL
	1 tablespoon	15 mL
	¼ cup	59 mL
	⅓ cup	79 mL
	½ cup	118 mL
	¾ cup	177 mL
	1 cup	237 mL
	2 cups (1 pint)	474 mL
	4 cups (1 quart)	1 L
	4 quarts (1 gallon)	4 L

WEIGHTS	½ ounce	14 g
	¾ ounce	21 g
	1 ounce	28 g
	2 ounces	57 g
	3 ounces	85 g
	4 ounces	113 g
	5 ounces	142 g
	6 ounces	170 g
	7 ounces	198 g
	8 ounces	227 g
	9 ounces	225 g
	10 ounces	283 g
	11 ounces	312 g
	12 ounces	340 g
	16 ounces (1 pound)	454 g

	FARENHEIT	CELSIUS
OVEN TEMPERATURES	300°	150°
	325°	165°
	350°	180°
	375°	190°
	400°	200°
	425°	220°
	450°	230°
	475°	245°
	500°	260°

TOP TRICKS

Brush up on these basic skills before you start.

HOW TO CRACK EGGS

1
Crack the egg on a flat, clean surface.

2
Use both hands to hold the egg over a bowl and gently pull the egg shell apart. The egg will drop into the bowl.

3
Discard the shells.

If eggshells fall into the bowl, don't stress. Use one half of the shell to scoop them out.

HOW TO LINE BAKING PANS AND SHEETS

1
Spray the pan with nonstick spray. This will help hold the parchment paper in place.

2
Pull the parchment paper across the pan to measure how much you will need.

3
Cut the parchment paper to the same size as the pan.

4
Insert the parchment paper and gently press down so it sticks to the pan.

Leave some parchment hanging over the edge so you can remove your baked goods with ease.

LEVEL 1

SLICING VEGETABLES

Prep steps are important, so take your time, especially when handling knives. Enlist an adult to be your chopping co-captain if you need while you are getting the hang of it.

Before you start, remember to stabilize your cutting board on a clean counter and curl your fingers or make a claw with your hand holding the vegetable so your fingers are safe from the blade.

HOW TO CUT INTO STICKS

1

Make a flat edge. Trim off the ends of the zucchini and slice it in half cross-wise. Working with one half, carefully use a chef's knife to slice a strip (about ¼-inch) off 1 side. Roll zucchini onto that side; this stabilizes the zucchini. Next, do the same thing 3 more times so you have a rectangle.

2

Cut planks, or slices. Cut thin wide strips (about ¼-inch thick).

3

Cut sticks. Working with 1 strip/plank at a time, cut into thin strips.

HOW TO DICE

1

Make flat edges.
Cut off the top and bottom of the pepper to make flat edges.

2

Cut around core. Rotate pepper with each cut each time (4 rotations). Discard core with seeds and pull away as much of the white ribs as possible.

3

Slice into strips. Flatten the pepper halves out and slice them into thin strips (about ¼–inch thick).

4

Cut cubes. Turn stack of sticks 90 degrees, hold them in place with one hand, and cut through to make small cubes.

1

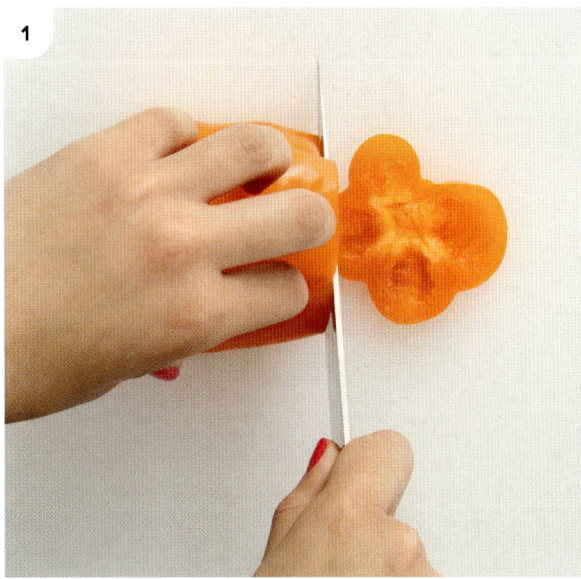

2

3

4

Cutting vegetables into just the right shape and size makes food cook quickly and evenly.

HOW TO CUT ROUND VEGETABLES

1

Cut off the stem end.
This creates a flat edge
and keeps the root end
intact (to help hold all the
onion's layers together).

2

**Cut the onion in half and
peel.** Stand the onion up
on its flat edge and cut
through the root to slice
the onion in two pieces.
Peel off the dry skins
until you get to the thick,
shiny onion underneath.

3

**Slice carefully into each
half.** Place onion half
cut-side down with the
root end pointing to
the back of the cutting
board. Cut slices through
all the layers of the
onion without cutting
through the root.

4

Rotate and chop. Turn
the onion so that the root
end points to the left
side of the cutting board
if you are right-handed
or to the right side of the
cutting board if you are
left-handed. Cut
perpendicularly through
the slices to make even,
little pieces of onion.
Stop chopping before you
get to the root end
(discard root).

1

i An onion has
two sides: the
root end (the one
with the little dried
"hairs") and the
stem end (shown
here).

2

3

4

HOW TO CUT SMALL ROUND VEGETABLES

1 Position your knife. Place the blade of a paring knife on
the top of the tomato, but don't cut through it just yet.
2 Stabilize it. Hold the tomato steady between your thumb
and index finger.
3 Cut through. Slice it into two pieces.

HOW TO MAKE HALF-MOONS

1

Clean and prep. Use a vegetable peeler to remove the outer skin of the carrot.

2

Make flat edges. Trim off the ends of carrot to make two flat edges.

3

Cut it lengthwise. Lay carrot flat on cutting board. Cut carrot crosswise in half. Working with one half, put tip of chef's knife onto board. Hold carrot between thumb and fingers, and cut carrot into two pieces.

4

Cut half-moons. Lay carrot halves cut-side down. Thinly slice the carrot halves, moving from top to bottom, to make half-moons.

Learn more about peeling on

P. 32

WHAT YOU'LL NEED

- ○ Chef's knife
- ○ Cutting board
- ○ Measuring cups and spoons
- ○ Small spoon
- ○ Butter knife
- ○ Medium bowl
- ○ Whisk

Learn how to pit an avocado on p. 44

TOTAL TIME
45 MINUTES

SERVES 4

Cucumber Sushi

Traditional maki rolls wrap vegetables and proteins in rice and seaweed, but here veggies are wrapped in... another veggie, a crisp cucumber! This is the time to focus on your knife skills and make careful, even cuts. The more time you spend preparing your veggies, the better the colorful reveal will be when you slice into the "sushi roll."

INGREDIENTS

- 2 medium English cucumbers, halved crosswise
- ¼ avocado, thinly sliced
- ½ red bell pepper, seeds and ribs removed, thinly sliced
- ½ yellow bell pepper, seeds and ribs removed, thinly sliced
- 2 small carrots, peeled, thinly sliced
- ⅓ cup mayonnaise
- 1 tablespoon sriracha (optional)
- 1 teaspoon soy sauce

DIRECTIONS

1 Using a small spoon, remove seeds from center of cucumbers until hollow.

2 Press avocado slices into center of cucumber, using a butter knife to press down inside cucumber. Slide in bell peppers and carrots until cucumber is full of veggies.

3 In a medium bowl, whisk mayonnaise, sriracha (if using), and soy sauce until combined.

4 Slice cucumber into 1–inch–thick rounds. Serve with sauce alongside.

WHAT MAKES CUCUMBERS ENGLISH?

Sometimes called hothouse cucumbers, these cucumbers are longer and thinner with smaller seeds. English cucumbers are also a little firmer and sweeter than other cucumbers and have ridged skin that does not require peeling, making them ideal for this recipe.

WHAT YOU'LL NEED

- Chef's knife
- Cutting board
- Measuring cups and spoons
- Large mixing bowl
- Mixing spoon
- Small mixing bowl
- Whisk

TOTAL TIME
25 MINUTES

SERVES 4

30

Greek Salad (Horiatiki)

This chunky, bright salad has no lettuce! That's right, the combination of juicy tomatoes, crispy cucumbers, briny olives, and a simple vinaigrette has been a traditional Greek side for a long, long time. People in different parts of Greece add other ingredients, like green bell peppers. This version, with tangy feta, originated in Athens in the 1960s and is the most popular in the United States.

INGREDIENTS

- 1 seedless cucumber, thinly sliced into half-moons
- ½ red onion, thinly sliced
- 2 cups grape or cherry tomatoes, halved
- 1 cup halved pitted Kalamata olives
- 6 ounces feta, cut into small cubes (about ½ inch)
  Juice of ½ lemon
- 2 tablespoons red wine vinegar
- 1 teaspoon dried oregano
  Kosher salt
  Freshly ground black pepper
- ¼ cup extra-virgin olive oil

DIRECTIONS

1 In a large bowl, mix cucumber, onion, tomatoes, and olives. Sprinkle feta over top and gently stir to combine.

2 In a small bowl, whisk lemon juice, vinegar, and oregano until combined; season with salt and pepper. Slowly drizzle in oil, whisking until dressing is combined and smooth.

3 Drizzle dressing over salad and toss to combine.

ARE RAW ONIONS JUST TOO MUCH?

Try soaking the slices in warm water for 10 to 15 minutes, then rinse with cold water, drain, and pat them dry before mixing them into your salad. This mellows out their bite.

PEELING

Some fruits and vegetables have outer skins that are tough, hard to clean, and sometimes not delicious to eat. Use a peeler to cut only the thin outer layer off the food.

TOOLBOX

PEELERS

There are three types of peelers.

Y peelers are great for tough skins and large fruits/vegetables.

Swivel peelers are just that—they move with the contours of the fruit/vegetable. They are good for delicate, thin skins.

Straight peelers have a stationary blade and are a good all-around peeler.

1
Stabilize the food.
Hold the food steady with one hand and use the other hand to position the vegetable peeler on the skin of the food.

2
Press down and pull.
Gently press down on the handle of the vegetable peeler and pull the peeler away from you against the food to remove the skin.

3
Rotate and continue peeling. Rotate the food and reposition your steadying hand as you continue to peel.

2

3

Make sure the blade is safely distanced (at least 1 inch) from your fingers.

WHAT YOU'LL NEED

o Measuring cups and spoons

o Vegetable peeler

o Large mixing bowl

o Rubber spatula

o Large rimmed baking sheet

o Tongs

o Oven mitts

TOTAL TIME
30 MINUTES

SERVES 2 TO 4

USE YOUR SKILL

Veggie Peel Chips

Before you toss those peels, make them into a crispy snack!
We made these with potatoes and carrots, but you can try them
with beet and/or apple peels.

INGREDIENTS

3 cups packed peels,
   such as russet potatoes,
   sweet potatoes,
   and/or large carrots (see
   sidebar)

1 tablespoon
   extra–virgin olive oil

1 tablespoon everything
   bagel seasoning

DIRECTIONS

1 Preheat oven to 425°F. In a large bowl, use a
   rubber spatula to toss peels, oil, and seasoning
   until coated. Spread peels in an even layer on a
   large baking sheet.

2 Bake peels, tossing halfway through and watching
   carefully during the last few minutes, until golden
   brown and crisp, 10 to 15 minutes. Let cool on
   baking sheet.

EVEN STRIPS MAKE GREAT CHIPS

Wash the vegetables well before peeling to
remove any dirt or debris; dry them well so the
peels aren't wet. Then, using a vegetable peeler,
peel the vegetables into long, thick strips
rather than small bits. Smaller ones will crisp
and darken faster than bigger ones.

WHAT YOU'LL NEED

- ○ Measuring cups and spoons
- ○ Vegetable peeler
- ○ Chef's knife
- ○ Cutting board
- ○ Spoon
- ○ Large saucepan
- ○ Wooden spoon
- ○ Immersion blender or food processor
- ○ Four 8-ounce heatproof resealable containers

TOTAL TIME
1 HOUR AND
20 MINUTES

SERVES 4

USE YOUR SKILL

Apple Butter

Apple butter is similar to applesauce, but you cook the apples longer for a stronger flavor and a thicker, smoother sauce. Top warm pancakes or biscuits with it or spread the sweet, fruity condiment on a cheddar cheese sandwich.

INGREDIENTS

- 2 pounds apples (about 6)
- 2 cups water
- ¼ cup (50 grams) granulated sugar
- Juice of 1 lemon
- ½ teaspoon ground cinnamon
- ¼ teaspoon ground nutmeg

DIRECTIONS

1 Using a vegetable peeler, peel skins off apples. Cut each apple in half lengthwise. Using a spoon, scoop out core and seeds; discard. Cut apple halves into small cubes.

2 Transfer apples to a large saucepan. Add water, sugar, lemon juice, cinnamon, and nutmeg. Bring to a boil over medium-high heat, then reduce heat to medium-low and simmer, stirring occasionally, until apples are softened and liquid is reduced, 40 to 50 minutes.

3 Using an immersion blender or food processor, blend mixture until very smooth.

4 Pour apple butter into 4 (8-ounce) resealable containers and let cool to room temperature. Refrigerate for up to 5 days.

WHAT APPLES SHOULD I USE?

All apples work well here! Using a variety of apples will only make the flavor more complex.

GALA
With rosy skin and juicy sweetness, this classic has great flavor and color.

MACINTOSH
Also a go-to that brings tartness and a softer texture.

JONAGOLD
Crunchy and tangy, this apple adds refreshing acidity.

FUJI
This crisp and juicy apple is also mildy sweet.

GOLDEN DELICIOUS
This tender variety offers more concentrated sweetness.

PREPPING CITRUS

Oranges, lemons, limes, and grapefruits are juicy and have "pulp"—little seed-like bits that store the juice. Citrus fruits can be amazing in recipes if you know the right way to prep and slice them.

RASP GRATER

BOX GRATER

TOOLBOX

GRATERS

There are two types of graters. Rasp graters are great for zesting citrus and grating Parmesan. You can also use the smallest holes on a box grater.

1

2

HOW TO ZEST

The "zest" is the outer skin of the citrus—and it adds great flavor without adding watery juice. There are a few ways to zest, but make sure to only remove the bright, colorful peel and not the white "pith" underneath the skin (it's bitter).

1
Position your grater.
Pull rasp grater against citrus fruit skin. Hold the citrus fruit in one hand and use a rasp grater to remove just the outermost layer of colorful skin.

2
Tap to release.
Once collected in the grater, tap the rasp against the cutting board to release the zest.

HOW TO JUICE

To get the most out of the citrus, roll the fruit around to loosen it up first, slice it open, and squeeze out the juice.

1
Position your knife. Place the blade on the top of the citrus fruit, but don't cut through just yet. Arch your other hand up and over the positioned knife, with your thumb stabilizing one side of the citrus fruit and your other four fingers stabilizing the other side.

2
Cut the citrus fruit. Cut through the center to make two pieces.

3
Squeeze out the juice. Use citrus press or your hands to squeeze the juice out of the citrus fruit into a small bowl. Use a spoon or strainer to remove seeds.

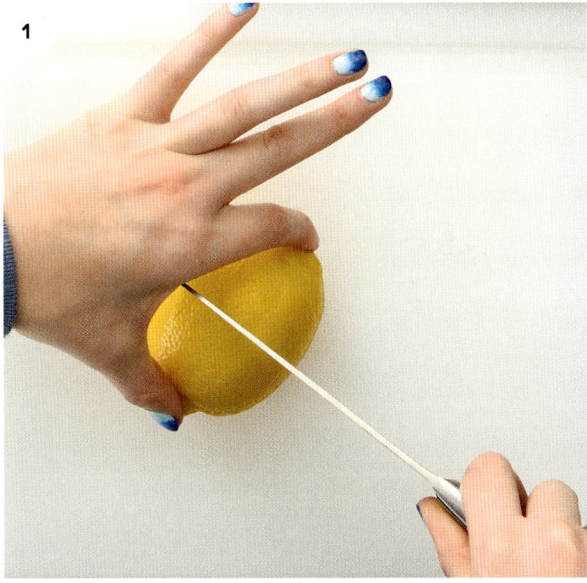

1

CITRUS PRESS

CITRUS REAMER

TOOLBOX

JUICERS

To get the most juice out with ease, try a reamer or citrus press. A press will even even separate out the seeds for you!

2

3

WHAT YOU'LL NEED

○ Measuring cups and spoons

○ Blender

○ 8-inch square baking dish

○ Fork

○ 6 small serving bowls or glasses

TOTAL TIME
15 MINUTES, PLUS FREEZING TIME

SERVES 6

USE YOUR SKILL

Granita

This tropical mix of pineapple and citrus juices is sweet and refreshing. Granita is an ultra-cool frozen Italian dessert made by partially freezing a mixture of fruit and juice (or another sweetened liquid) and then using a fork to scrape and break up the icy crystals. Basically, it's homemade shaved ice!

INGREDIENTS

- 2 cups frozen pineapple chunks
- ½ cup fresh orange juice (from 1 to 2 oranges)
- ¼ cup (55 grams) packed dark brown sugar
- 2 teaspoons fresh lime juice (from 1 lime)
- 1 teaspoon pure vanilla extract

  Kosher salt

  Store-bought whipped cream, toasted coconut flakes, and finely chopped fresh pineapple, for serving

DIRECTIONS

1 In a blender, blend frozen pineapple, orange juice, brown sugar, lime juice, vanilla, and a pinch of salt until smooth, about 2 minutes. Let rest for 1 minute to settle, then continue to blend until pineapple is pureed and smooth and sugar is dissolved.

2 Pour pineapple mixture into an 8-inch square baking dish. Freeze, uncovered, until starting to get icy but not totally frozen, about 2 hours.

3 Using a fork, scrape icy bits together and stir mixture well. Continue to freeze until almost frozen solid, about 2 hours more.

4 Again, using fork, scrape mixture into icy pieces. Continue to freeze until completely frozen solid, about 1 hour more.

5 Divide granita among 6 small serving bowls or glasses. Top with whipped cream, toasted coconut, and fresh pineapple.

A NECESSARY INTERRUPTION

For the best slushy, icy granita, you have to do something you are generally told not to do: You have to interrupt the ice crystals. By removing the dish from the freezer to scrape and stir the mixture the granita changes from a iquid to a solid. This prevents the ice crystals from freezing and makes a scoopable, semi-frozen treat.

WHAT YOU'LL NEED

- Measuring cups and spoons
- 9-inch round cake pan
- Parchment paper
- Zester
- Chef's knife
- Cutting board
- Paring knife
- Large mixing bowl
- Whisk
- Spatula
- Cake tester or wooden skewer
- Oven mitts
- Wire rack
- Large serving platter

TOTAL TIME
1 HOUR AND
35 MINUTES

SERVES 8

Citrus Upside-Down Cake

The coolest thing about this cake is that you build it upside down! Arrange the citrus (you can use any combination you'd like), pour in the cake batter, and pop it into the oven. When it is done baking (and has cooled, of course), flip it over onto a platter and reveal the shiny, jewel–like citrus top.

Learn to line a pan with parchment on

P. 21

INGREDIENTS

Cooking spray

3–4 citrus fruits, such as grapefruits, navel oranges, and/or blood oranges

2 tablespoons unsalted butter, melted, cooled slightly

½ cup (100 grams) granulated sugar

2 large eggs

1 (13.25–ounce) box yellow cake mix

1 cup fresh orange juice

⅓ cup vegetable oil

DIRECTIONS

1 Preheat oven to 350°F. Grease a 9-inch round cake pan with cooking spray, then line with parchment.

2 Zest 1 navel orange (you should have about 1 tablespoon zest) and set aside. Slice both the zested orange and remaining citrus fruits into ¼-inch–thick round slices. Using a paring knife, remove peel and pith from around edges.

3 Pour butter into the bottom of prepared pan and sprinkle with sugar. Arrange grapefruit and orange wheels on top, slightly overlapping so bottom is completely covered (you may not use all of the fruit).

4 In a large bowl, whisk eggs until blended. Add cake mix, orange juice, oil, and reserved zest and whisk until combined. Pour batter over arranged fruit and carefully spread into an even layer.

5 Bake cake until a tester inserted into the center comes out clean, 40 to 50 minutes. (The cake may sink slightly in the center, and this is okay.) Transfer pan to a wire rack.

6 Let cake cool 15 to 20 minutes. Using oven mitts, invert cake onto a platter. Let cool completely.

PITTING FRUITS

Fruits such as mangoes, peaches, plums, and nectarines have large, hard, inedible pits in the middle. You can't cut through the pit, so you have to cut around it.

HOW TO PIT A PEACH

1
Cut halfway through the fruit.
Gently cut through the fruit until the knife reaches the pit.

2
Rotate and repeat. Carefully remove the knife and rotate the fruit. Repeat steps 1 and 2 to cut through the fruit to the pit from the other side. You will have one slice going all the way around the fruit from top to bottom.

3
Twist. Place one hand on each side of the slice in the fruit and gently twist in opposite directions to separate the fruit into two pieces.

4
Remove the pit. Use a spoon (or your fingers) to remove and discard the pit.

2

4

ALL FRUITS CONTAIN SEEDS

Sometimes they are tiny seeds, like in the case of strawberries, and sometimes a fruit has one big seed (also called a pit), like a peach. Believe it or not, avocados and olives also fall into this category of pitted fruits.

HOW TO CUT A MANGO

1

Position the mango.
Cut a thin slice from the bottom of the mango. (This stabilizes it.) Stand the mango up tall so the stem is facing up.

2

Position your knife.
Place your knife blade on the top center of the mango, then move it ½ inch to the side (so you are no longer over the pit that runs lengthwise through the center of the fruit). Hold the mango steady with your other hand and slice half of the mango off the pit. Rotate the remaining mango and slice the other side off the pit. Discard the pit.

3–4

Score the mango flesh.
Place the mango halves skin–side down on the cutting board. Use a paring knife to score the flesh (cut through the flesh but not through the skin) to make a checkered pattern.

5

Flip it inside out. Pick up the mango half and push from underneath to flip it inside out.

7

Remove cubes. Use a spoon to remove the mango cubes from the skin.

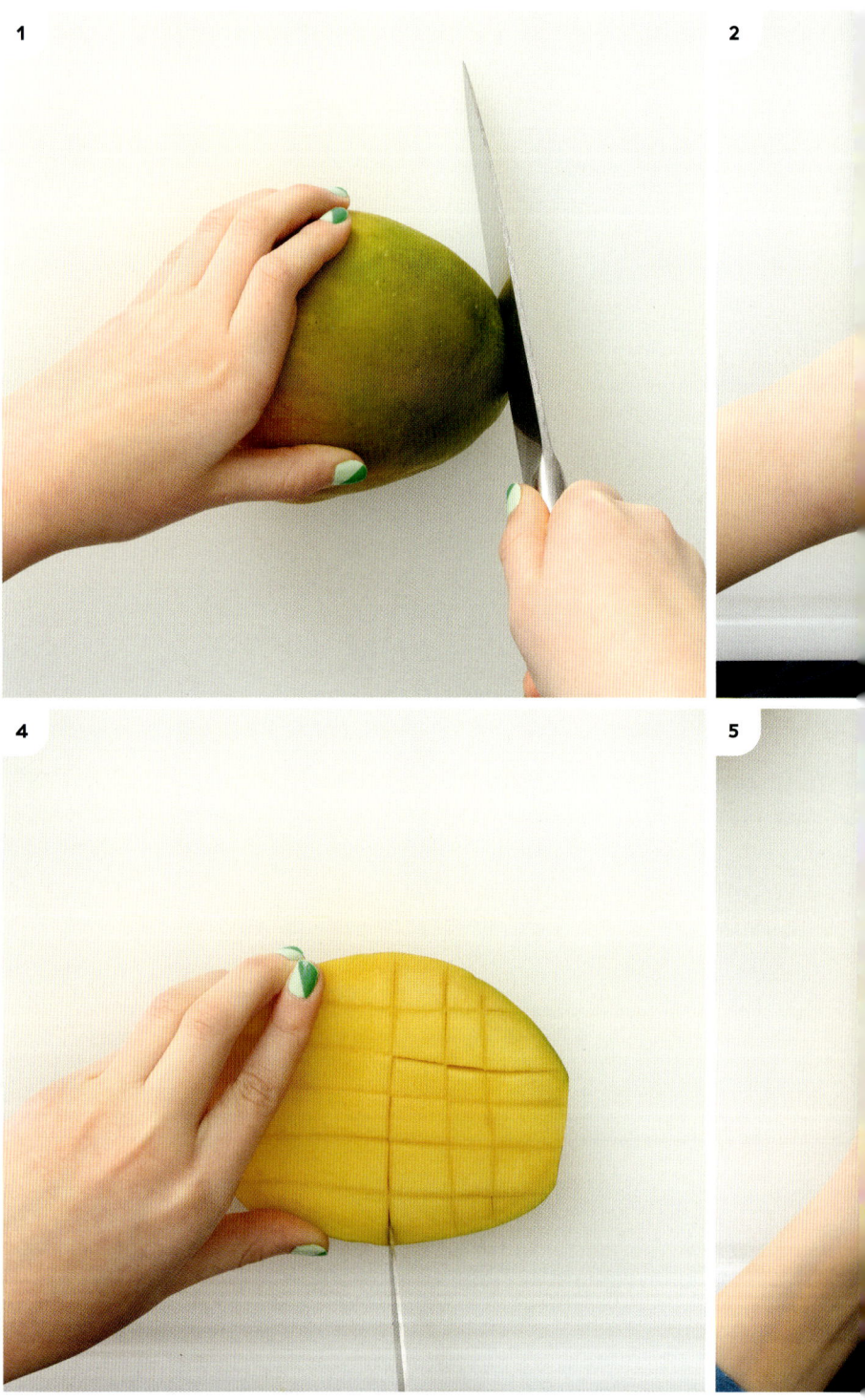

Never try to cut through a mango pit! Instead cut around it.

3

6

WHAT YOU'LL NEED

- ○ Measuring cups and spoons
- ○ Paring knife
- ○ Large saucepan
- ○ Heatproof spoon
- ○ Slotted spoon
- ○ Cutting board
- ○ Blender
- ○ Fine–mesh sieve
- ○ Medium mixing bowl
- ○ Spatula
- ○ 4 dessert bowls
- ○ Ice cream scoop

FRESH OR FROZEN?

If you're making this out of peach season, use defrosted frozen peach slices. Raspberries are available year–round, so be sure to stick with fresh for this recipe.

TOTAL TIME
30 MINUTES

SERVES 4

USE YOUR SKILL

Peach Melba Sundae

There is nothing better than seasonal fruit for dessert, especially when it's paired with ice cream! This take on peach melba continues the tradition of pairing peaches with a fresh tart raspberry sauce and vanilla ice cream.

INGREDIENTS

- 4 ripe peaches
- 4 cups water
- 2 cups (400 grams) granulated sugar
- ½ cup (60 grams) confectioners' sugar
- 1 teaspoon fresh lemon juice
- 3 cups fresh raspberries, divided

  Vanilla ice cream, for serving

DIRECTIONS

1 Using a paring knife, score an X into the bottom of each peach to help with peeling later. In a large saucepan over high heat, bring water and granulated sugar to a boil, stirring until sugar is dissolved. Add peaches and reduce heat to medium-low. Simmer, stirring occasionally, until peaches are tender, 6 to 10 minutes. Using a slotted spoon, transfer peaches to a cutting board and let cool slightly.

2 Meanwhile, in a blender, blend confectioners' sugar, lemon juice, and 2 cups raspberries on high speed until well combined, about 1 minute. Strain through a fine-mesh sieve into a medium bowl, using a spatula to help push sauce through the sieve (you should have about ¾ cup raspberry sauce). Discard seeds.

3 When peaches are cool enough to handle, peel and discard skin. Cut peaches in half and discard pits. Cut each half into 4 wedges.

4 Divide peach slices among bowls. Scoop ice cream into bowls. Drizzle with raspberry sauce and top with remaining 1 cup raspberries.

WHAT YOU'LL NEED

- Knife
- Cutting board
- Measuring cups and spoons
- Large mixing bowl
- Wooden spoon

TOTAL TIME
30 MINUTES

SERVES 4

USE YOUR SKILL

Mango Salsa

This will be your new fave snack! This chunky salsa is equal parts sweet, spicy, and salty, and you can change it up until you find your perfect combination. Not a fan of heat? Leave out the jalapeño or substitute chopped green bell peppers. Want to up the heat? Add even more jalapeño or some poblano chiles for extra spice and a smoky flavor.

INGREDIENTS

1   ripe mango, pitted, diced

1   ripe avocado, pitted, diced

¼   red onion, peeled, diced

1   small jalapeño, seeds and ribs removed, diced

1   cup grape tomatoes, quartered

Juice of 1 lime

2   tablespoons chopped fresh cilantro

2   teaspoons extra-virgin olive oil

Kosher salt

Tortilla chips, for serving

DIRECTIONS

In a large bowl, combine mango, avocado, onion, jalapeño, tomatoes, lime juice, cilantro, and oil; season with salt. Toss gently to combine. Serve with chips alongside. If you have leftovers, store in an airtight container and refrigerate for 3 to 5 days.

HOW TO CHOP HERBS

Roll your fresh cilantro sprigs up into a tight bundle. Hold onto the stems of the bundle with one hand and use a chef's knife to finely chop the leaves.

SLICING + PREPPING MEAT

Always prep raw meat on a clean, stable cutting board with enough room so it doesn't touch any of the other ingredients.

HOW TO CUBE CHICKEN BREAST

1–2
Slice. Stabilize the meat with one hand and insert a sharp knife into the meat. Pull your knife through the meat to slice it.

3
Cube. Slice strips into 1–inch cubes.

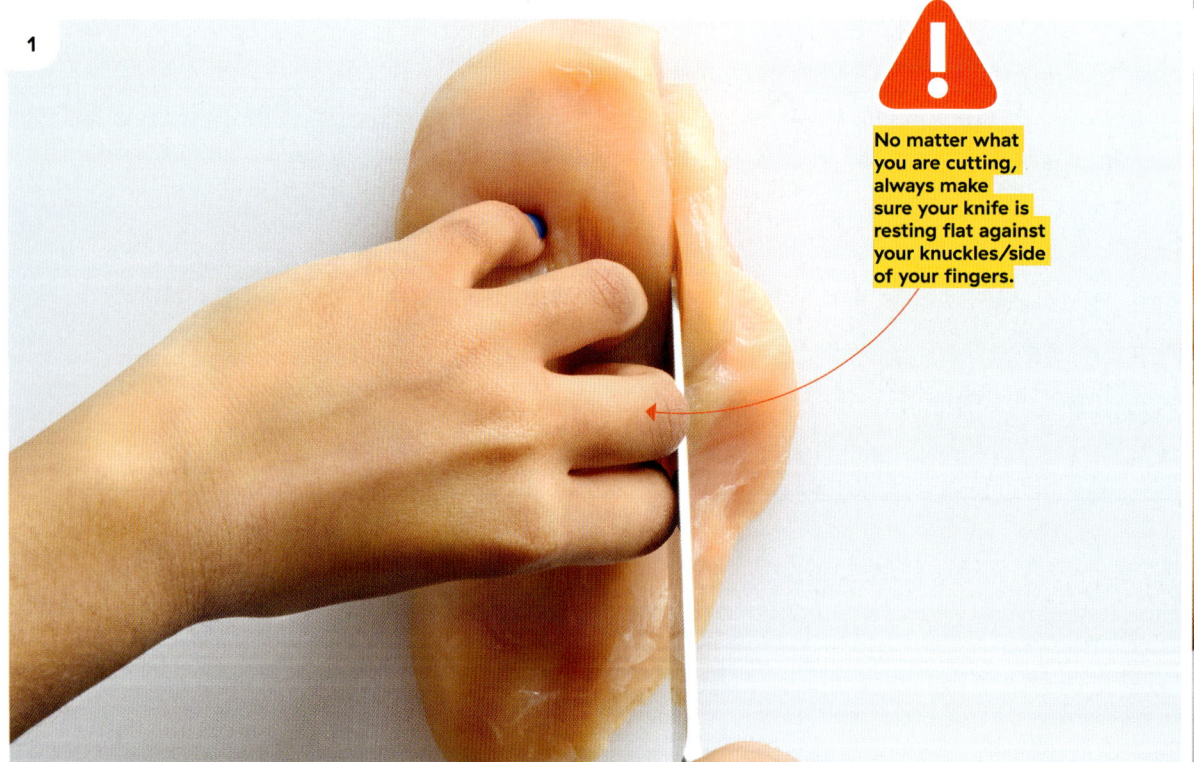

No matter what you are cutting, always make sure your knife is resting flat against your knuckles/side of your fingers.

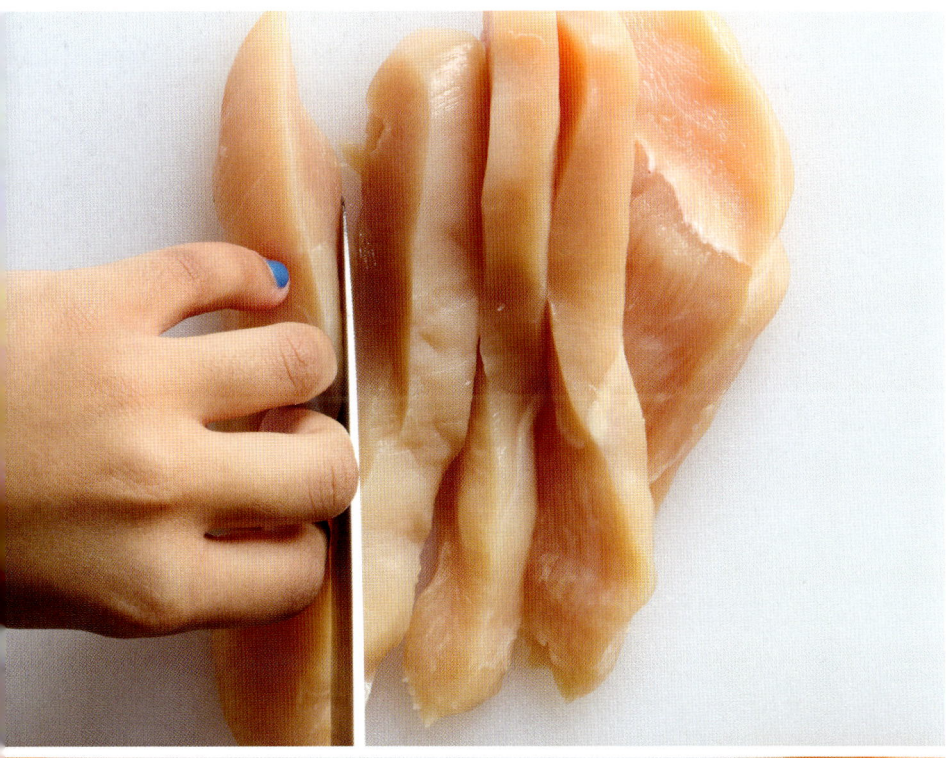

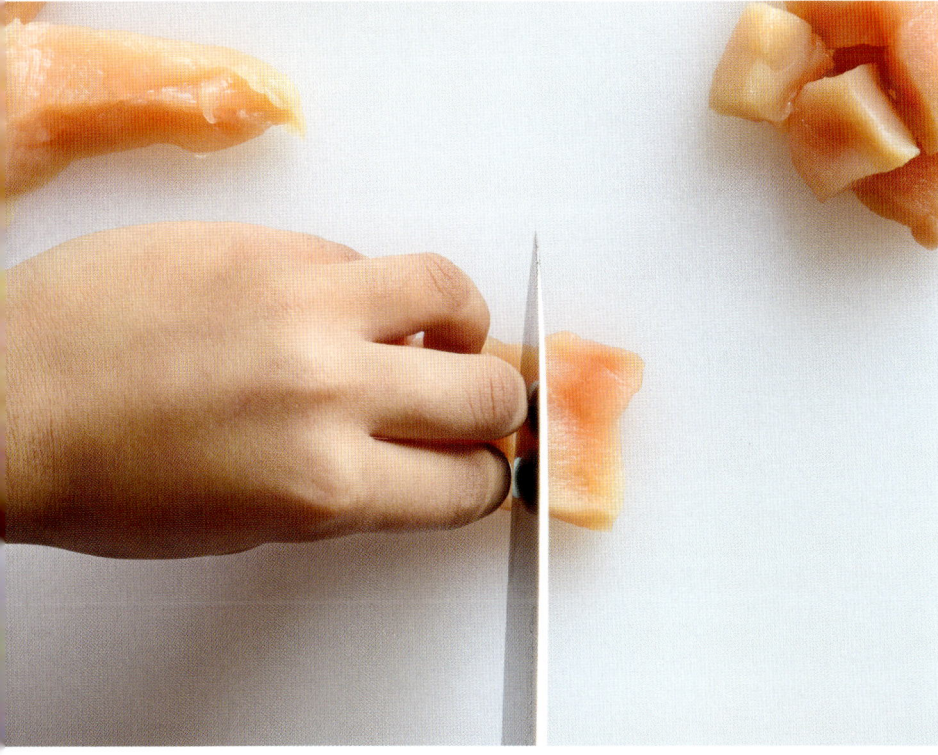

3 WAYS TO AVOID CROSS CONTAMINATION

Raw meat needs careful handling because tiny, invisible bacteria can hop from it to just about any surface, creating all sorts of mischief—including potentially making people sick. This is called cross contamination. To stay safe, follow these important steps:

WASH HANDS

Immediately after touching the raw meat, wash your hands with soap and warm water.

CLEAN UP

Clean the cutting board, knife, and counter with warm, soapy water before moving onto the next step in your recipe.

SAFELY STORE MEAT

Transfer the prepped meat to either a cooking vessel or a clean storage container.

WHAT YOU'LL NEED

- Measuring spoons
- Cutting board
- Knife
- Small mixing bowl
- Small spoon
- Wooden spoon
- Large skillet

TOTAL TIME
40 MINUTES

SERVES 4

Chicken Tacos

Put the premade taco seasoning packet away—trust us, it's worth it! These Americanized tacos load up corn tortillas with seasoned chicken made with a quick homemade spice blend. Serve these on your next Taco Tuesday (or Wednesday, or Thursday...) with any variety of toppings, including the Mango Salsa on page 51!

INGREDIENTS

FOR THE TACOS

2 teaspoons chili powder

2 teaspoons ground cumin

½ teaspoon garlic powder

¼ teaspoon cayenne (optional)

¼ teaspoon paprika

3 tablespoons (or more) extra-virgin olive oil

4 boneless, skinless chicken breasts, cut into 1-inch strips

   Kosher salt

   Freshly ground black pepper

8 corn tortillas, warmed

FOR THE TOPPINGS

Sour cream

Diced tomatoes

Shredded Monterey Jack

Diced avocados

Lime wedges

DIRECTIONS

1 In a small bowl, combine chili powder, cumin, garlic powder, cayenne (if using), and paprika.

2 In a large skillet over medium heat, heat oil. Season chicken with salt and black pepper and cook, stirring occasionally (about once every minute), until golden brown and cooked through, about 6 minutes. Add spice mixture and cook, stirring and adding a little more oil or water if needed, until chicken is coated, about 1 minute more.

3 Divide chicken among tortillas. Top with desired toppings. Serve with lime wedges alongside.

HOW TO WARM TORTILLAS IN A SKILLET

Heat a skillet over high heat and arrange your tortillas in a single layer. Toast, flipping occasionally, until warm and pliable.

WHAT YOU'LL NEED

- o Measuring spoons
- o Large rimmed baking sheet
- o Aluminum foil
- o Wire rack
- o 3 shallow mixing bowls
- o Whisk
- o Tongs
- o Small mixing bowl
- o Ovens mitts
- o Large serving platter

TOTAL TIME
45 MINUTES

SERVES 4

USE YOUR SKILL

Cornflake Chicken Tenders

Chicken and waffle lovers will flip for these sweet and salty tenders and the maple–mustard dipping sauce.

INGREDIENTS

- 1 cup (120 grams) all-purpose flour
- Kosher salt
- Freshly ground black pepper
- 2 large eggs
- 3 tablespoons pure maple syrup, divided
- 2 cups crushed Cornflakes
- 1½ pounds boneless, skinless chicken breasts, sliced into 1-inch strips
- ¼ cup Dijon mustard

DIRECTIONS

1 Preheat oven to 400°F. Line a large rimmed baking sheet with foil and place a wire rack on top.

2 In a shallow bowl, season flour with salt and pepper. In another shallow bowl, beat eggs and 1 tablespoon maple syrup to combine. In a third shallow bowl, season Cornflakes with salt and pepper.

3 Coat chicken first in flour shaking off excess, then in egg mixture, letting excess drip off, then in Cornflakes, gently pressing to adhere. Transfer to prepared rack. Bake until chicken is cooked through and coating is crispy and golden, about 25 minutes.

4 Meanwhile, in a small bowl, mix mustard with remaining 2 tablespoons maple syrup.

5 Arrange chicken on a platter. Serve with maple mustard alongside.

CRUSH IT!

Place the cereal in a resealable bag and push as much air out as you can before sealing it. Then roll over the bag with a rolling pin to crush the cereal into crumbs.

LEVEL 2

Pureeing

TOMATO SOUP + DOLE WHIP SMOOTHIE BOWLS

P. 60

Prepping Garlic

PESTO + GARLIC KNOTS

P. 66

Whisking

BIRTHDAY CAKE DIP + DALGONA-STYLE WHIPPED CHOCOLATE

P. 72

Grating

ZUCCHINI BREAD + GIANT SKILLET LATKE

P. 78

Frying Eggs

FRICO FRIED EGG TOSTADA + PESTO EGG-IN-A-HOLE

P. 84

PUREEING

When you want to change a food's texture to make it smooth, blend it in a blender or puree it in a food processor.

1

Fill it up. Place ingredients in a food processor or blender.

2

Close lid. Make sure the lid is tightly closed. If using a food processor, make sure the lid is fully clicked into the locked position.

3

Blend. Turn the food processor or blender on to process or blend until smooth.

TOOLBOX

BLENDER VS. PROCESSOR

Both appliances have powerful motors and sharp blades to puree food. If your mixture is more of a liquid, use a blender. If you want a thicker blend, use a food processor.

⚠️ If you are pureeing something hot, make sure to let it cool down a few minutes before blending. If there's too much steam in the blender, the lid might pop off and hot food could jump out and make a mess or, even worse, burn your hand.

WHEN DO I PULSE?

If you want to chop something up but don't want it completely smooth in texture (think about homemade salsa—you still want to have little pieces of tomato, onion, and peppers), use the pulse button by pushing it down for 1–second increments. Continue pulsing the food until it reaches the desired choppy texture.

3

WHAT YOU'LL NEED

- Chef's knife
- Cutting board
- Measuring spoons and cups
- Large pot
- Wooden spoon
- Blender
- Large heatproof mixing bowl
- 4 to 6 soup bowls

HOW TO STORE
Keep the leftover soup in an airtight container for up to 3 days. To reheat, pour soup into a pot on the stove over medium-low heat or place in a bowl and microwave, stopping and stirring every 30 seconds.

TOTAL TIME
1 HOUR

SERVES 4 TO 6

Tomato Soup

Move over, grilled cheese. This tomato soup is a superstar!
Three forms of tomatoes—tomato paste,
whole tomatoes, and tomato juice—and a splash of heavy cream
create a rich, robust blend with big flavor.

INGREDIENTS

- 4 tablespoons unsalted butter
- 2 stalks celery, thinly sliced
- ½ yellow onion, thinly sliced
- ½ small fennel bulb, thinly sliced
- 2 teaspoons kosher salt, divided
- 2 tablespoons tomato paste
- ¼ teaspoon crushed red pepper flakes (optional)
- 2 (28–ounce) cans whole peeled tomatoes
- 1½ cups tomato juice (from a 12–ounce can)
- 1 tablespoon light brown sugar
- ½ cup heavy cream, plus more for drizzling
- ¼ cup fresh basil leaves

DIRECTIONS

1 In a large pot over medium heat, melt butter. Add celery, onion, fennel, and ½ teaspoon salt and cook, stirring occasionally, until softened and translucent, 7 to 8 minutes. Add tomato paste and cook, stirring frequently, until darkened, about 2 minutes. Add red pepper flakes (if using) and cook, stirring, until fragrant, about 1 minute more.

2 Add whole tomatoes with their juices, tomato juice, and brown sugar. Bring to a simmer, mashing down on tomatoes with a wooden spoon to break into large pieces, and cook, stirring occasionally, until slightly reduced, about 10 minutes. Let cool slightly, about 5 minutes.

3 Transfer half of tomato mixture to a blender and blend until smooth. Pour blended soup into a large bowl and repeat with remaining tomato mixture. Return soup to pot and stir in cream. Cook over medium heat, stirring frequently, just until warmed through (do not let it boil); season with remaining 1½ teaspoons salt.

4 Divide soup among bowls. Drizzle with cream and top with basil.

WHAT IS FENNEL?

It's a vegetable that tastes like...licorice! There are three parts of the fennel plant: the bulb, the stalk, and the bright green fronds. All of them are edible, but we are just using the bulb in this recipe.

WHAT YOU'LL NEED

- ○ Chef's knife
- ○ Cutting board
- ○ Measuring cups
- ○ Blender
- ○ 3 bowls

TOTAL TIME
20 MINUTES

SERVES 3

Dole Whip Smoothie Bowls

Slurping smoothies with a straw is great, but a smoothie in a bowl is more fun because...toppings!

INGREDIENTS

- 1 banana, peeled, sliced, plus more for serving
- 1½ cups frozen pineapple chunks, plus more, thawed, for serving
- 1 cup unsweetened coconut milk
- ¼ cup shredded coconut, toasted

  Maraschino cherries (optional)

DIRECTIONS

1 In a blender, blend banana, pineapple, and coconut milk on high speed until smooth.

2 Divide smoothie among 3 bowls. Top with more pineapple chunks, banana slices, and coconut. Garnish with cherries (if using).

HOW TO TOAST COCONUT

1 Preheat oven to 325°F.

2 On a large rimmed baking sheet, spread coconut in a single layer.

3 Bake, stirring every 3 minutes with a heatproof spatula, until golden brown and smells toasty, 6 to 10 minutes.

WHAT IS COCONUT MILK?

Coconut milk is made by mixing grated coconut meat with water. After it's strained, the "milk" is thick and rich with fats and flavor. It's usually sold in cans and often has a thick layer of coconut cream on top (make sure to stir it all together!). This is different from coconut water, which is the clear liquid found inside a young green coconut.

PREPPING GARLIC

Garlic cloves are each wrapped in a thin skin. They grow in a cluster, called a garlic "head." An outer paper-like skin wraps the whole bulb together.

1

Separate the cloves. Peel the outer skin off the garlic head to reveal individual pieces.

2

Smash to loosen skins. Place a clove on your cutting board and carefully use your knife with the blade facing away from you to lightly smash the clove and loosen the skins from the garlic. Remove and discard the skins.

3

Trim and chop. Use a knife to trim off the hard, tough end of the clove and chop according to your recipe specifications.

GARLIC SPROUTS

You might notice a little green sprout growing out of the top of your garlic clove. Don't worry! That sprout is edible and just means the clove is starting to regenerate. If the garlic clove is firm and white, it's still good to eat. Watch out for soft, mushy, browned cloves—those are too old and should be discarded.

!

Always keep your other hand far away from the sharp side of the blade!

HOW TO MINCE GARLIC

Use a rocking motion with your chef's knife. Gently rock the blade from tip to base over the garlic clove again and again until you have evenly sized small bits of chopped garlic.

WHAT YOU'LL NEED

- ○ Chef's knife
- ○ Cutting board
- ○ Measuring cups
- ○ Box grater
- ○ Food processor
- ○ Medium mixing bowl
- ○ Rubber spatula

HELP! I DON'T HAVE A FOOD PROCESSOR!

Traditionally pesto was made using a marble mortar and a wooden pestle, so if you happen to have one, you're in business. You can also chop everything by hand; just make sure your knife is nice and sharp. A dull blade can bruise the basil and make it turn brown.

TOTAL TIME
25 MINUTES

MAKES 1 CUP

68

USE YOUR SKILL

Pesto

Put the store-bought jar down. Bursting with fresh basil flavor, homemade pesto is easy to create (5 ingredients and 15 minutes!) and incredibly versatile. Once you've mastered this classic recipe, the sky is the limit—there are countless variations.

INGREDIENTS

- 2 cups tightly packed fresh basil leaves
- ½ cup extra-virgin olive oil
- ¼ cup pine nuts
- 2 cloves garlic, finely chopped

  Kosher salt
- ½ cup finely grated Parmesan

DIRECTIONS

1 In a food processor, pulse basil, oil, pine nuts, garlic, and a large pinch of salt until smooth.

2 Transfer basil mixture to a medium bowl and stir in Parmesan; season with more salt, if needed. Keep in an airtight container and refrigerate up to 1 week.

MIX IT UP!

Create your own ideal pesto by mixing up these ingredients.

NUTS

Almonds, pistachios, walnuts, or even pecans are all great substitutions, but you can also use seeds like sunflower or pumpkin seeds.

CHEESE

If you're looking to stray from the classic Parmesan, any hard, salty aged cheese will work best. We like Pecorino or Manchego.

GREENS

You can either swap out the basil completely or go 50/50 with arugula, kale, or mint.

HOW ELSE CAN YOU USE PESTO?

Spread it on pizza dough or drizzle it on your eggs!

▶▶

Try Pesto Egg-in-a-Holes on

P. 89

WHAT YOU'LL NEED

- ○ Measuring cups and spoons
- ○ Box grater
- ○ Chef's knife
- ○ Cutting board
- ○ 2 baking sheets
- ○ Parchment paper
- ○ Small saucepan
- ○ Pizza wheel or sharp knife
- ○ Ruler
- ○ Pastry brush
- ○ Oven mitts
- ○ Large bowl
- ○ Large serving platter

TOTAL TIME
50 MINUTES

MAKES 15

Garlic Knots

Garlicky, herby, and slathered in butter—yes, please! These knots use store-bought pizza dough as a quick shortcut. But how do you tie them? No stress; we will take you through it step by step.

INGREDIENTS

1   (1-pound) package store-bought pizza dough

½   cup (1 stick) unsalted butter

6   cloves garlic, finely chopped or grated

½   teaspoon kosher salt

    All-purpose flour, for surface

2   tablespoons fresh parsley, finely chopped

¼   cup finely grated Parmesan

DIRECTIONS

1 Let dough sit on the counter until it's room temperature. Place a rack in center of oven; preheat to 400°F. Line 2 baking sheets with parchment.

2 In a small saucepan over low heat, melt butter. Add garlic and salt and cook, stirring frequently, until starting to froth, about 5 minutes. Immediately remove saucepan from heat. Let cool.

3 On a lightly floured surface, stretch dough into a rectangle about 12 inches by 10 inches. Using a pizza wheel or sharp knife, cut rectangle into quarters, then cut each quarter vertically into 4 equal strips about 6 inches long. Roll each strip into a rope and tie into a knot, tucking ends into the center.

4 Arrange knots on prepared sheets, spacing at least 1 inch apart. Brush with about one-third of garlic butter. (Try to avoid using pieces of garlic, as they may burn in the oven.)

5 Bake garlic knots, rotating sheets halfway through, until golden brown, 15 to 20 minutes.

6 Meanwhile, stir parsley into remaining garlic butter. (If butter has solidified, briefly reheat on the stove.)

7 Transfer knots to a large bowl. Add garlic butter and toss to coat. Arrange on a platter, then top with Parmesan.

HOW TO MAKE KNOTS

1
Stretch the dough out into a rectangle.

2
Cut the rectangle into quarters, then cut each quarter vertically into 4 equal strips.

3
Roll each strip into a rope.

4
Tie each rope into a knot.

5
Tuck the ends into the center.

SKILL
WHISKING

When you want to combine two or more substances into one smooth mixture or incorporate air into ingredients (hello whipped cream!) use a whisk.

1

Pour everything into a large bowl.
Place your ingredients in a large bowl. You'll need plenty of room so your ingredients don't fly out of the bowl! Use one hand to stabilize it.

2-3

Whisk side to side. Make quick, continuous, side-to-side motions, moving the whisk around the bottom of the bowl. This incorporates air into the ingredients, making everything fluffy.

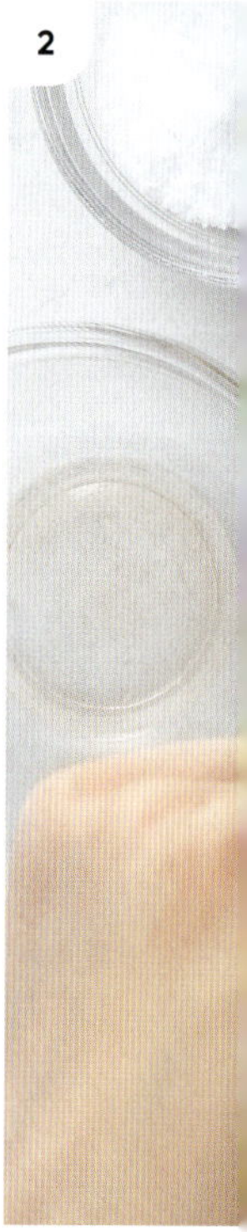

1

3

HANDHELD MIXER

STAND MIXER

TOOLBOX

MIXERS

If you have a hand–held electric mixer or a stand mixer, you can use it in steps 2–3. If using a stand mixer, fit it with the whisk attachment.

WHAT ABOUT WHIPPING?

Some ingredients like cream and egg whites begin to hold their shape when you whisk them for a long time. You'll learn more about whipping in Level 5!

WHAT YOU'LL NEED

- Measuring spoons and cups
- Large mixing bowl
- Whisk
- Rubber spatula
- Serving bowl

HOW TO STORE

Keep dip in an airtight container and refrigerate for up to 3 days. Bring to room temperature before serving.

TOTAL TIME
15 MINUTES

SERVES 5

USE YOUR SKILL

Birthday Cake Dip

This is cake in dip form! A fluffy mixture of butter, cream cheese, confectioners' sugar, and crunchy confetti sprinkles, this vanilla buttercream frosting–inspired snack is great with vanilla wafers, fruit, or pretzels.

INGREDIENTS

- ½   cup (1 stick) unsalted butter, room temperature
- 4   ounces cream cheese, room temperature
- 2   teaspoons pure vanilla extract
- 2   cups (230 grams) confectioners' sugar
- ¼   cup sprinkles

     Vanilla wafer cookies, for serving

DIRECTIONS

1   In a large bowl, whisk butter and cream cheese until light and fluffy, about 3 minutes (the mixture will be quite stiff and slow to mix at first; just keep whisking!). Whisk in vanilla, then gradually add confectioners' sugar and whisk until combined, about 1 minute. Using a rubber spatula, mix in sprinkles.

2   Transfer dip to a serving bowl. Serve with cookies alongside.

HOW CAN I MAKE THIS FOR A VEGAN FRIEND?

That's easy! Substitute cream cheese and butter for vegan alternatives.

WHAT YOU'LL NEED

- ○ Measuring spoons and cups
- ○ Medium mixing bowl
- ○ Whisk
- ○ 8-ounce juice glass
- ○ Spoon

TOTAL TIME
5 MINUTES

SERVES 1

USE YOUR SKILL

Dalgona-Style Whipped Chocolate

Hot chocolate just got even cooler. This iced beverage has layers of flavors and textures. Instead of instant coffee, which is what is used in the classic Korean dalgona, it uses Nesquik cocoa powder to create a foamy chocolate milk topper.

INGREDIENTS

- 3 tablespoons Nesquik chocolate–flavored powder
- 2 tablespoons heavy cream

  Ice
- ½ cup whole, 2%, or skim milk

DIRECTIONS

1 In a medium bowl, whisk Nesquik and cream until mixture thickens and doubles in size; it should hold firm peaks like whipped cream.

2 Fill an 8–ounce juice glass with ice. Pour milk over ice. Spoon whipped Nesquik mixture over top.

KEEP IT STEADY

You don't want your bowl spinning around as you whisk. If you're having trouble keeping the bowl steady with one hand, try rolling up a kitchen towel and forming it into a circular nest. Place your bowl on top of the towel nest for increased stability while you whisk.

SKILL
GRATING

To get even, small shreds of an ingredient, use a grater. A box grater has 4 sides with holes for different types of shreds. If you aren't sure which side to use, go ahead and grate a couple practice strokes to see how they turn out.

1

Position the grater and food. Place a box grater on a clean cutting board. Hold it steady with one hand gripping the top handle. Hold the food perpendicular to the grater with the other hand, making sure your fingers are tucked far away from the sharp holes on the grater. Keep the food at a 90-degree angle against the grater.

GLOVE WORK

If you'll be doing a lot of grating, you might want to get some cut-resistant gloves. Unlike thin plastic gloves, cut-resistant gloves are thick and can protect your fingertips from getting injured on the sharp edges of the grater.

2

Drag food down grater. Apply some pressure and drag the food from the top of the grater down to the bottom. These long strokes ensure nice, even shreds. It is also the most efficient way to use all the holes on the grater.

3

Rotate and repeat. Repeat, rotating the food as necessary so your fingers don't get too close to the grater, until most of the ingredient has been grated.

The holes of your box grater can become dull with frequent use. They can't be sharpened, so it's best to replace it when needed.

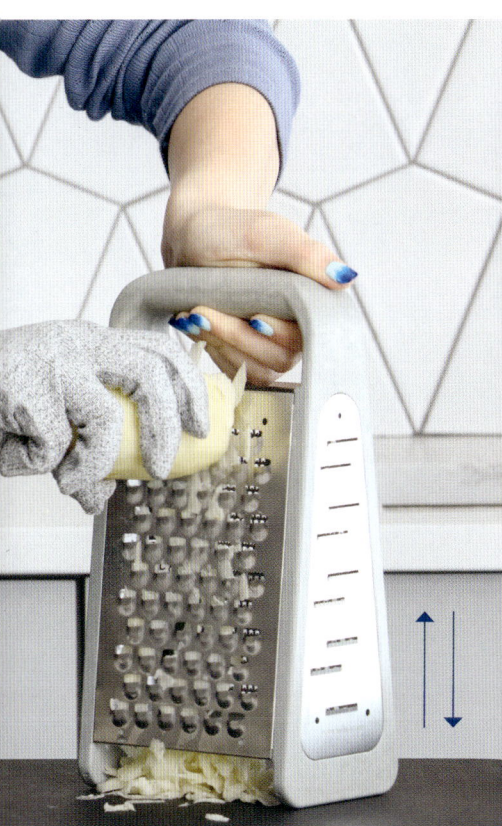

79

WHAT YOU'LL NEED

- Measuring cups and spoons
- Box grater
- 9-inch-by-5-inch loaf pan
- Medium mixing bowl
- Whisk
- Large mixing bowl
- Rubber spatula
- Cake tester or wooden skewer

TOTAL TIME
1 HOUR AND 50 MINUTES

SERVES 8 TO 10

USE YOUR SKILL

Zucchini Bread

If you like banana bread, try zucchini bread! This squash-filled quick bread has a crunchy top and is soft as can be inside, perfect for enjoying for breakfast or as an afternoon pick-me-up.

INGREDIENTS

Cooking spray

2½ cups (300 grams) all-purpose flour

1 teaspoon baking powder

1 teaspoon ground cinnamon

¾ teaspoon kosher salt

½ teaspoon baking soda

¾ cup (160 grams) packed light brown sugar

½ cup (100 grams) granulated sugar

½ cup (1 stick) unsalted butter, melted, cooled

½ cup vegetable oil

3 large eggs

1 teaspoon pure vanilla extract

3½ cups grated zucchini (from 2 large or 3 medium)

DIRECTIONS

1 Preheat oven to 350°F. Grease a 9-inch-by-5-inch loaf pan with cooking spray. In a medium bowl, whisk flour, baking powder, cinnamon, salt, and baking soda.

2 In a large bowl, whisk brown sugar, granulated sugar, butter, and oil until combined. Add eggs and vanilla and mix until smooth. Add dry ingredients and fold until just a few streaks remain. Add zucchini and mix until just combined. Pour batter into prepared pan; smooth top.

3 Bake bread until a tester or wooden skewer inserted into the center comes out clean, about 1 hour 15 minutes. Let cool completely before slicing. Zucchini bread will stay fresh, wrapped tightly in an airtight container, for up to 5 days. It can also be wrapped and stored in a freezer-safe container in the freezer for up to 3 months. Thaw at room temperature before slicing.

DOUBLE DUTY

This simple recipe is also a perfect way to practice whisking! But take care to not overmix—it will make your bread dense.

WHAT YOU'LL NEED

- ○ Box grater
- ○ Large mixing bowl
- ○ Measuring cups and spoons
- ○ Clean kitchen towel or nut milk bag
- ○ 10-inch non-stick skillet, preferably cast iron
- ○ Rubber spatula
- ○ Pastry brush
- ○ Oven mitts
- ○ Large plate
- ○ Large serving platter

TOTAL TIME
45 MINUTES

SERVES 6

Giant Skillet Latke

Latkes are fried potato pancakes often made to celebrate Hanukkah, but they are good all year round! To achieve a latke's signature golden edge and crispy bite, take the extra step and squeeze out the potato shreds' extra moisture with a kitchen towel.

INGREDIENTS

5   medium russet potatoes (about 2 pounds total), peeled, halved crosswise

1   medium yellow onion, peeled

1   large egg, lightly beaten

¼   cup matzo meal

1½   teaspoons kosher salt

½   teaspoon freshly ground black pepper

3   tablespoons extra-virgin olive oil, plus more for brushing

Flaky sea salt

Sliced chives, sour cream, applesauce, and/or crème fraîche, for serving

DIRECTIONS

1   Preheat oven to 425°F. Coarsely shred potatoes and onion on the large holes of a box grater.

2   Line a large bowl with a clean kitchen towel or nut milk bag. Transfer potatoes and onions to prepared bowl. Squeeze out excess liquid from potatoes and onions, leaving liquid in bowl.

3   Carefully pour out liquid from bowl, keeping leftover potato starch, which should be stuck to bottom of bowl. Transfer potatoes and onions to a bowl with remaining potato starch. Add egg, matzo meal, kosher salt, and pepper, and mix until well combined.

4   Preheat a 10-inch nonstick skillet, preferably cast iron, over medium-high heat until hot, about 1 minute. Pour in 3 tablespoons oil and heat until a small piece of potato mixture sizzles when added.

5   Add potato mixture to skillet and firmly pat down to compact with a rubber spatula. Using a pastry brush, carefully brush top with about 2 teaspoons oil (this will ensure a golden exterior).

6   Use oven mitts to transfer skillet to oven. Bake latke until golden brown and edges are crispy, about 15 minutes. Grab an adult and oven mitts and carefully invert latke onto a plate, then slide back into skillet. Continue to bake until other side is golden brown, 7 to 10 minutes more.

7   Sprinkle with sea salt. Top with chives. Serve in skillet or on a platter with toppings alongside.

TOPPINGS WE LOVE A LATKE

Applesauce and sour cream are iconic choices, but you can put anything on a latke! Switch it up with Apple Butter (page 37) or some apricot or strawberry jam. We like the maple-mustard dipping sauce on page 57 too!

FRYING EGGS

A perfectly cooked fried egg can upgrade practically anything, from avocado toast to a double cheeseburger and beyond.

1
Crack egg. Break egg into a small bowl or cup.

2
Melt butter. In a small nonstick skillet, melt butter over medium heat until frothy.

3
Cook. See cook times at right.

4
Season and serve. Transfer fried egg to a plate; season with salt and pepper.

WHAT KIND OF PAN IS BEST FOR FRYING EGGS?

Nonstick, all the way. Or seasoned cast-iron skillet. But make sure to still use some butter and/or oil so they slide right out.

1

3

2

4

HOW DO YOU LIKE YOUR EGGS?

SUNNY-SIDE UP

Cook, undisturbed, until white is completely set, about 3 minutes.

OVER-EASY

Cook, undisturbed, until white is just set, about 2 minutes. Flip and cook until white is completely set, about 30 seconds more.

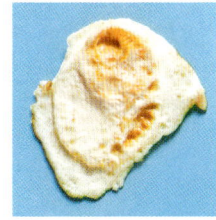

OVER-HARD

Cook, undisturbed, until white is fully set, about 3 minutes. Flip and cook until yolk is completely set, 2 to 3 minutes more.

WHAT YOU'LL NEED

- Chef's knife
- Cutting board
- Measuring cups and spoons
- Medium mixing bowl
- Spoon
- Rimmed baking sheet
- Parchment paper
- Small mixing bowl
- Small nonstick skillet with lid
- Nonstick spatula

TOTAL TIME
45 MINUTES

SERVES 4

i

WHAT'S A FRICO?

Fricos, or cheese crisps, are a popular treat in northern Italy, where they're eaten as snacks. While they're traditionally made with Montasio cheese, any other hard or semi-firm cheese can be used, including Parmesan, Gruyère, or cheddar.

USE YOUR SKILL

Frico Fried Egg Tostadas

Heads up, fried egg lovers: Your favorite breakfast just got a serious upgrade. Featuring a base of crispy caramelized cheddar and pepper Jack cheese (frico) and a zesty pico de gallo topping, these cheesy frico fried egg tostadas will surpass your wildest breakfast expectations—and might even become your new favorite dinner.

INGREDIENTS

1   large tomato, cored, finely chopped

½   jalapeño, seeded, finely chopped

¼   red onion, finely chopped

2   tablespoons chopped fresh cilantro

2   tablespoons fresh lime juice

½   teaspoon kosher salt, plus more for seasoning

2   ounces cheddar, shredded (about ½ cup)

2   ounces pepper Jack cheese, shredded (about ½ cup)

4   large eggs

    Freshly ground black pepper (optional)

DIRECTIONS

1   In a medium bowl, combine tomato, jalapeño, onion, cilantro, and lime juice; season with ½ teaspoon salt. Set aside until ready to serve.

2   Line a rimmed baking sheet with parchment. In a small bowl, mix cheddar and pepper Jack until combined.

3   In a small nonstick skillet, spread ¼ cup cheese mixture in an even circular layer. Cook over medium heat, undisturbed, until cheese is melted and bubbling, 1 to 2 minutes.

4   Crack 1 egg into center of cheese; season with salt and pepper, if desired. Cook, undisturbed, until egg white is almost set and frico is a deep orange–brown, about 2 minutes. Cover pan (in a pinch, you can cover with a piece of foil) and continue to cook until egg white is set, about 1 minute. Uncover and continue to cook until frico is firm enough to lift, about 1 minute more.

5   Using a nonstick spatula, carefully transfer frico to prepared sheet. Let sit 2 minutes to let frico harden. Repeat with remaining cheese mixture and eggs.

6   Serve topped with pico de gallo.

- o Measuring spoons

- o Bread knife

- o Cutting board

- o Cup or paring knife

- o Small nonstick skillet

- o Spatula

- o Plate

TOTAL TIME
10 MINUTES

SERVES 1

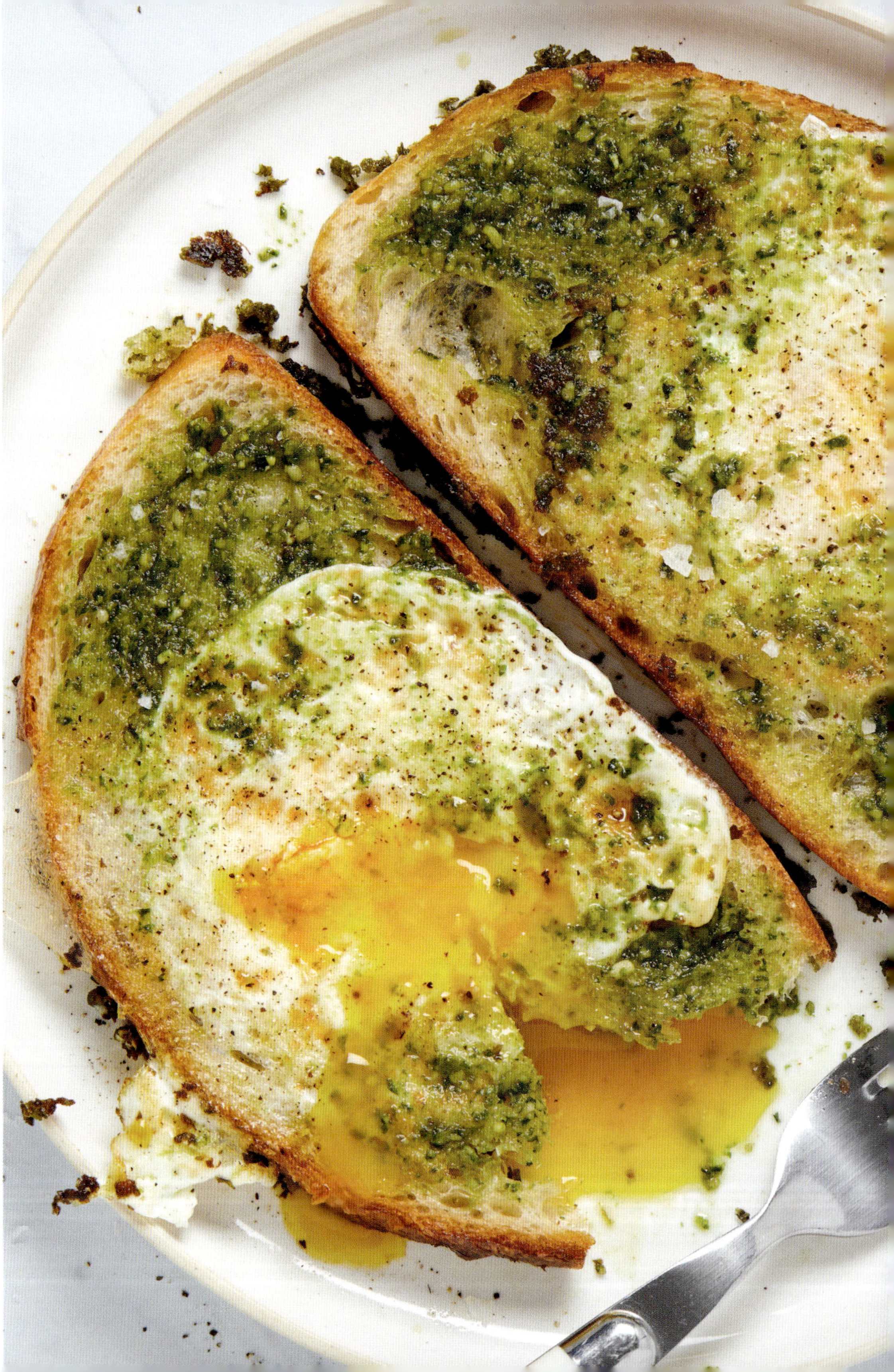

Pesto Egg-in-a-Hole

What's better than an egg and toast? An egg IN toast.
Pesto does double duty: Its oily base keeps the egg from sticking
to the pan, and it delivers delicious herby flavor.

INGREDIENTS

1 (1-inch-thick) slice bread, such as ciabatta or sourdough

1 tablespoon pesto, store-bought or homemade (page 69)

1 large egg

Kosher salt

Freshly ground black pepper

DIRECTIONS

1 Using a cup or paring knife, cut an egg-sized hole in the center of bread; enjoy cut-out bread as a chef's snack.

2 In a small nonstick skillet over medium heat, heat pesto until lightly sizzling. Add bread, then crack egg into hole in bread. Cook 3 minutes, flip, and cook 1 minute more for an over-easy egg.

3 Transfer bread to a plate; season with salt and pepper.

SUPERB SANDWICH

Make this breakfast into another favorite: a sandwich! Layer a toasted slice of bread with bacon, sausage or ham, cheese of choice, and top with a Pesto-Egg-in-A-Hole.

LEVEL 3

Steaming

PERFECT STEAMED ASPARAGUS + STEAMED BLOOMING CUPCAKES

P. 92

Boiling + Straining

MAC + CHEESE PIZZA BITES + CACIO E PEPE

P. 98

Sautéing

PHILLY CHEESESTEAKS + MEXICAN BEEF & RICE SKILLET

P. 104

Searing

CHICKEN FRIED RICE + SMASH BURGERS

P. 110

Shallow Frying

TOASTED RAVIOLI + PARMESAN ZUCCHINI FRITTERS

P. 116

STEAMING

To cook food without submerging it, perch ingredients above boiling water (using a steamer basket) and let steam do the cooking. This method preserves nutrients and color vibrancy in fruits and vegetables.

1

Boil a little water. Place a small amount of water in a pot or pan and bring it to a boil over medium heat.

2

Steam. Once boiling, place the ingredient in a metal or silicone basket or bamboo tray.

3

Cook. Lower in basket and cover it with a lid to trap the steam inside. This will gently cook the food. Cook food following your recipe instructions. Then turn off heat.

4

Carefully uncover. Remove the lid and release the steam.

WHAT IS AN ICE BATH?

Once the steam has settled down, remove food from the steamer basket. To rapidly cool the vegetable, prepare an ice bath: Before steaming, add about 2 cups ice to a large bowl, and fill bowl about halfway with cold water. Lift vegetables and drop into bowl, letting sit for about 1 minute.

2

4

⚠️ Uncover the pot away from you, tilting the lid so the steam releases on the other side. Keep your hands away from the top of the pot: the steam can be very hot!

WHAT YOU'LL NEED

- Paring knife
- Large skillet with lid
- Steamer basket
- Wooden spoon
- Large serving platter

TOTAL TIME
15 MINUTES

SERVES 2

USE YOUR SKILL

Perfect Steamed Asparagus

When cooked just right, asparagus is perfectly tender without becoming mushy or bland. Transform this springtime vegetable into a superstar side with just a little steam and two classic ingredients: butter and lemon.

INGREDIENTS

1   pound asparagus, trimmed

2   tablespoons unsalted butter, melted

     Kosher salt

     Freshly ground black pepper

     Lemon wedges, for serving

DIRECTIONS

1   Pour in water to just cover the bottom of a large skillet. Arrange asparagus in a single layer in a steamer basket. Set basket in skillet and bring water to a boil over medium heat. Cover and let steam until asparagus is easily pierced with a knife, 3 to 5 minutes.

2   Toss asparagus with butter; season with salt and pepper. Transfer to a platter. Serve with lemon wedges alongside.

HOW DO I TRIM ASPARAGUS?

Forget the knife; you can do this with your hands! Hold the asparagus stalk horizontally. Grab the center of the stalk with one hand and the thick bottom of the stalk with the other hand. Bend the stalk until the bottom snaps and discard.

WHAT YOU'LL NEED

- Large pot
- Steamer basket
- Measuring spoons and cups
- Large mixing bowl
- Whisk
- 2-ounce ice cream scoop
- 9 silicone cupcake molds
- Paring or butter knife
- Cake tester or wooden skewer
- Tongs
- Large plate
- Large serving platter

TOTAL TIME
40 MINUTES

MAKES 9

Steamed Blooming Cupcakes

Steaming might not be your first thought when it comes to making cupcakes, but hear us out—it's a fun method worthy of trying! Use a steamer basket to make these cupcakes bloom, and once cool, serve them with a maraschino cherry in the center.

INGREDIENTS

1   large egg

¾   cup (150 grams) granulated sugar

2   cups Original Bisquick™ mix

⅔   cup whole milk

2   tablespoons unsalted butter, melted

2   teaspoons pure vanilla extract

20 drops pink gel food coloring

    Cooking spray

9   maraschino cherries, stems removed

DIRECTIONS

1   Fill a large pot with 2 to 3 inches water. Set a steamer basket over water.

2   In a large bowl, whisk egg and sugar until combined. Add Bisquick, milk, butter, vanilla, and food coloring and whisk until well combined.

3   Scoop batter into 9 silicone cupcake molds (do not spray molds with cooking spray or the cupcakes won't "bloom"). Spray a paring or butter knife with cooking spray and cut an "X" into one of the cupcakes. Wipe off knife, spray again, and continue until every cupcake has an "X" on top.

4   Arrange molds in steamer basket, spacing at least 1 inch apart. Bring water to a boil over medium–high heat. Cover pot and steam, adding more water as needed to ensure pot doesn't dry up, until cupcakes bloom and a cake tester or wooden skewer inserted into the center comes out clean, 12 to 15 minutes. Using tongs, transfer cupcakes to a plate and let cool.

5   Arrange cupcakes on a platter. Place a cherry in the center of each before serving.

SILICONE MOLD

TOOLBOX

ALTERNATIVE LINERS

Similar to cupcake liners, silicone molds are sturdier; they are available online and can be reused in place of liners in your favorite cupcake recipes.

BOILING + STRAINING

Cooking food directly in hot water is called boiling. While it's a straightforward process, it can be quite dangerous. Following these steps will ensure you are safe.

1
Bring water to a boil. Fill a pot half to three–quarters full with water. This will go much faster if you cover the pot with a lid.

2
Cook ingredient(s). Carefully add your ingredient(s) to the pot. Quickly remove your hand from above the pot after adding ingredient(s) to avoid getting splashed with hot water.

3
Prepare colander. While your food is boiling, set a colander in a large bowl. This will catch any excess water from the food.

4
Strain. Use tongs to remove your food and place in the colander.

2

Always be careful when handling a pot of boiling water. Ask an adult for help if the pot is too heavy or if it feels too hot for you to carry on your own.

4

WHAT YOU'LL NEED

- Chef's knife
- Cutting board
- Muffin tin
- Wooden spoon
- 2 large pots
- Ladle
- Measuring cups and spoons
- Heatproof liquid measuring cup
- Whisk
- Rubber spatula
- Colander
- Spoon
- Oven mitts

TOTAL TIME
1 HOUR AND
15 MINUTES

MAKES 12

USE YOUR SKILL

Mac + Cheese Pizza Bites

Pizza, pasta, or both? Both, please! Creamy mac, pepperoni, and plenty of Parmesan combine to create a bite-size snack that we can't stop eating.

INGREDIENTS

- 16 large slices pepperoni, divided
- Kosher salt
- 8 ounces elbow pasta
- 4 tablespoons unsalted butter
- ¼ cup (30 grams) all-purpose flour
- 1¼ cups milk
- ½ cup heavy cream
- 1 teaspoon dried oregano
- 1 teaspoon garlic powder
- Freshly ground black pepper
- 2 cups shredded mozzarella
- ¾ cup finely grated Parmesan, divided
- Torn fresh basil, for serving

DIRECTIONS

1 Preheat oven to 400°F. Cut a small slit into the side of 12 pepperoni slices. Arrange a slice in each cup of a standard 12-cup muffin tin. Chop remaining 4 slices of pepperoni into small pieces; set aside.

2 In a large pot of boiling salted water, cook pasta, stirring occasionally, until al dente according to package directions. Using a ladle, carefully scoop out some pasta cooking water. Pour ½ cup pasta water into a heatproof liquid measuring cup and set aside (discard any extra water you scooped up). Drain pasta in a colander.

3 Meanwhile, in another large pot over medium heat, melt butter. Add flour and whisk until golden, about 2 minutes. While whisking, slowly pour in milk. Add cream, oregano, and garlic powder; season with salt and pepper. Bring to a simmer and cook, stirring, until liquid is slightly thickened and reduced, about 2 minutes.

4 Remove from heat. Add mozzarella and ½ cup Parmesan and stir until cheese is melted.

5 Add 2 tablespoons reserved pasta water to cheese sauce and stir to combine. Add pasta and toss to coat, adding more pasta water as needed to loosen sauce.

6 Spoon macaroni mixture into pepperoni cups. Top with 2 tablespoons Parmesan and reserved chopped pepperoni.

7 Bake pizza bites until tops are golden and macaroni feels firm, 20 to 30 minutes.

8 Remove cups from tin. Top with basil and remaining 2 tablespoons Parmesan.

WHAT YOU'LL NEED

- Measuring cups and spoons
- Large pot
- Wooden spoon
- Ladle
- Heatproof liquid measuring cup
- Colander
- Large skillet
- Whisk
- Tongs

HOW TO BLOOM PEPPER

To "bloom" the spice, you'll fry freshly ground pepper in fat (here, oil and butter) to deepen the flavor.

TOTAL TIME
30 MINUTES

SERVES 2

USE YOUR SKILL

Cacio E Pepe

Cacio e pepe literally means "cheese and pepper" and it's a classic Italian combo. There are plenty of both in this simple Italian dish. Go the extra mile and use freshly ground pepper and freshly grated Parmesan and Pecorino. Trust us, it's worth it.

INGREDIENTS

Kosher salt

8 ounces linguine or spaghetti

2 tablespoons unsalted butter, divided

1 tablespoon extra–virgin olive oil

Coarsely ground black pepper

¾ cup finely grated Parmesan, plus more for serving

¾ cup finely grated Pecorino, plus more for serving

DIRECTIONS

1 In a large pot of boiling salted water, cook pasta, stirring occasionally, until al dente according to package directions. Using a ladle, carefully scoop out some pasta cooking water. Pour ⅔ cup pasta water into a heatproof liquid measuring cup and set aside (discard any extra water you scooped up). Drain pasta in a colander.

2 In a large skillet over medium heat, melt 1 tablespoon butter, then add oil; season with a generous amount of black pepper. Toast, stirring, until fragrant, about 1 minute.

3 Add ⅓ cup reserved pasta water and bring to a simmer. Whisk in remaining 1 tablespoon butter. Using tongs, add pasta and toss to combine. Add Parmesan and Pecorino and cook, tossing constantly, until about half of cheese is melted, about 2 minutes.

4 Remove from heat and continue to toss, adding reserved pasta water as needed to loosen, until cheese is melted.

5 Serve topped with more Pecorino and Parmesan.

PASTA WATER IS YOUR BEST FRIEND

The water you cooked your pasta in is salty (because you seasoned it well) and starchy (thanks to the dried noodles from the box). This magical stuff is the backbone of this dish and will make your sauce smooth, glossy, and emulsified.

SAUTÉING

This cooking method is often the first step to developing flavor when following a recipe. To sauté, you cook ingredients (such as vegetables or ground meat) over high heat in a small amount of fat.

1

Heat the fat. Heat cooking fat (oil or butter) in a wide, shallow pan, like a skillet, over medium–high heat until it shimmers.

2

Cook and stir. Add ingredient(s) to the hot skillet and cook, stirring often with tongs, or rubber spatula, according to your recipe. Cook until food is softened, golden brown, or another cue from the recipe instructions you are following.

DON'T CROWD THE PAN

Make sure you select a big enough vessel so ingredients stay in a single layer. This ensures your food crisps and browns instead of steams.

i WHAT IS FOND?

You will find browned bits of food on the bottom of your skillet after sautéeing. Should you wash them out? Absolutely not! Those little browned bits are called "fond" and are loaded with flavor. They are often incorporated into sauces or the next cooking stage of your recipe.

WHAT YOU'LL NEED

- Chef's knife
- Cutting board
- Large skillet with lid
- Measuring spoons
- Wooden spoon
- Plate
- Serrated knife

TOTAL TIME
1 HOUR AND
5 MINUTES

SERVES 4

Philly Cheesesteaks

While the traditional sandwich contains just three ingredients (steak, onions, and cheese), there are many variations including adding sautéed bell peppers and mushrooms. We are team peppers, and we add them while you sauté the onions.

INGREDIENTS

2 tablespoons extra-virgin olive oil, divided

2 green bell peppers, seeds and ribs removed, thinly sliced

2 red bell peppers, seeds and ribs removed, thinly sliced

1 large yellow onion, thinly sliced

Kosher salt

1½ pounds sirloin steak, thinly sliced

Freshly ground black pepper

8 slices provolone

4 hoagie rolls

DIRECTIONS

1 In a large skillet over medium heat, heat 1 tablespoon oil. Add bell peppers and onion; season with salt. Cook, stirring often, until golden brown, 12 to 15 minutes. Transfer bell peppers and onion to a plate.

2 In same skillet over medium-high heat, heat remaining 1 tablespoon oil. Add steak and cook, turning occasionally, until lightly browned and cooked through, about 5 minutes; season with salt and pepper.

3 Return veggies to skillet and toss to combine with steak. Top with provolone. Cover and cook until cheese is melted, about 3 minutes more.

4 Using a serrated knife, cut into long side of each roll, being sure not to cut all the way through. Divide cheesesteak mixture among rolls.

WHO INVENTED THE PHILLY CHEESESTEAK?

Pat Olivieri, a hot dog vendor in an Italian neighborhood in Philadelphia, wanted something besides hot dogs for lunch. So one day in 1930, he grilled some beef from a local butcher and threw it in a hoagie bun. A nearby cab driver smelled the sandwich and asked for it, and the iconic sandwich found its first fan!

WHAT YOU'LL NEED

- Chef's knife
- Cutting board
- Measuring spoons
- Large skillet with lid
- Wooden spoon

TOTAL TIME
45 MINUTES

SERVES 4

USE YOUR SKILL

Mexican Beef + Rice Skillet

Spiced ground beef, flavorful rice, hearty beans, and lots of cheese all come together in a skillet for a quick one-pot dinner. Don't skip the green chiles: They are mild, sweet, and complement the smoky fire-roasted tomatoes well.

INGREDIENTS

- 1 tablespoon extra-virgin olive oil
- 1 large yellow onion, chopped
- 1 pound lean ground beef
- 1 cup white rice
- 1 (15-ounce) can black beans, rinsed, drained
- 1 (15-ounce) can fire-roasted tomatoes
- 1½ cups corn (fresh, frozen, or canned)
- 1 (4-ounce) can green chiles
- 1 tablespoon ground cumin
- 1 teaspoon (or more) chili powder
  Kosher salt
- 2 cups low-sodium chicken broth
- 1½ cups shredded cheddar and/or Monterey Jack
  Fresh cilantro, for serving

DIRECTIONS

1 In a large skillet over medium heat, heat oil. Add onion and cook, stirring, until translucent, about 2 minutes. Add beef and cook, breaking up with a wooden spoon, until no longer pink, about 6 minutes. Drain fat.

2 Move beef to one side of skillet and add rice to the other side. Cook, stirring but keeping beef and rice separate, until rice is toasted, about 5 minutes. Add beans, tomatoes, corn, chiles, cumin, and chili powder; season with salt. Taste and add more chili powder depending on spice preference, if needed.

3 Add broth and stir to combine. Bring to a simmer, cover, and cook, stirring occasionally, until slightly thickened and flavors have melded, about 20 minutes.

4 Top with cheddar and Monterey Jack and cover to let melt, 2 to 3 minutes.

5 Sprinkle with cilantro.

HAVE LEFTOVERS?

Wrap this filling up in a tortilla and you've got a burrito for lunch!

SEARING

Searing is a technique where the outside of a food is cooked at a high heat without moving—it creates a brown crust on meat and fish and gives the food a ton of flavor. Always use caution with hot oil; it splatters and can burn you.

1

Heat fat. Heat cooking fat (oil or butter) in a skillet (or Dutch oven) over high heat until it is extremely hot.

2

Cook without stirring. Add ingredient(s) to the hot skillet and cook, without moving, until the food develops a dark golden–brown crust. (You can use tongs to carefully lift up a corner of the food to peek at the color forming.)

3

Flip. Use tongs or a spatula to flip and repeat on the second side (if specified in your recipe).

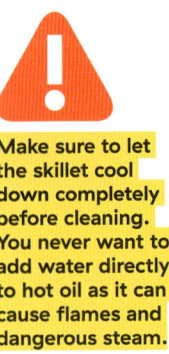

Make sure to let the skillet cool down completely before cleaning. You never want to add water directly to hot oil as it can cause flames and dangerous steam.

1

2

3

WHAT YOU'LL NEED

- Chef's knife
- Cutting board
- Measuring cups and spoons
- Medium skillet
- Wooden spoon

TOTAL TIME
50 MINUTES

SERVES 6

Chicken Fried Rice

If you have leftover rice hanging around in the fridge, rewarm in a pan with oil, soy sauce, and veggies to make a classic Chinese-American comfort food.

INGREDIENTS

- 4 tablespoons vegetable or canola oil, divided
- 3 (6- to 8-ounce) boneless, skinless chicken breasts
- Kosher salt
- Freshly ground black pepper
- 1 medium yellow onion, chopped
- 2 carrots, peeled, finely chopped
- 3 cloves garlic, finely chopped
- 1 tablespoon finely chopped peeled ginger
- 4 cups cooked white rice (preferably leftover)
- ¾ cup frozen peas
- 3 large eggs, beaten to blend
- 2 scallions, thinly sliced
- 3 tablespoons reduced-sodium soy sauce

DIRECTIONS

1. In a medium skillet over medium heat, heat 2 tablespoons oil. Season chicken with salt and pepper on both sides and cook, turning halfway through, until golden and no longer pink, about 8 minutes per side. Transfer to a cutting board, let rest 5 minutes, and cut into bite-size pieces.

2. In same skillet over medium-high heat, heat 1 tablespoon oil. Add onion and carrots and cook, stirring, until softened, about 7 minutes. Add garlic and ginger and cook, stirring, until fragrant, about 1 minute more. Stir in rice and peas and cook, stirring, until warmed through, about 2 minutes.

3. Push rice to one side of skillet and add remaining 1 tablespoon oil to the other side. Add eggs to oil and cook, stirring, until almost fully cooked through and set, about 2 minutes. Fold eggs into rice. Return chicken and any accumulated juices to skillet. Add scallions and soy sauce and stir to combine.

HOW TO PEEL GINGER

Use the side of a spoon to scrape the thin outer skin from a gnarly, knobby chunk of ginger root.

WHAT YOU'LL NEED

- Large cast-iron skillet or griddle
- Large metal spatula

TOTAL TIME
30 MINUTES

SERVES 4

USE YOUR SKILL

Smash Burgers

Super-thin patties and lacy, crispy edges are the chef's kiss of a smash burger. Give the ground beef a chance to really stick to the surface and form a crust by using an ungreased, piping-hot skillet or griddle. Since the skillet is so hot, the meat will still release easily when you are ready to flip the patties.

INGREDIENTS

1   pound lean ground beef

Kosher salt

Freshly ground black pepper

4   slices American cheese

Hamburger buns, mayonnaise, lettuce leaves, dill pickle slices, sliced tomatoes, and sliced onions, for serving

DIRECTIONS

1   Divide beef into 8 (2-ounce) pieces. Very loosely form patties into balls, making sure to not tightly pack together. Wash your hands before moving to the next step.

2   Heat an ungreased griddle or large cast-iron skillet over high heat until very hot. Working 2 or 4 at a time, depending on size of your griddle or skillet, place patties on hot griddle. Using a large metal spatula, immediately smash patties down as flat and thinly as you can; season with salt and pepper. Cook, undisturbed, until edges start to crisp, about 1 minute. Flip, season with salt and pepper, and cook until other side is browned, about 30 seconds.

3   Top half of patties with a slice of cheese, then top with a second cooked patty. Continue to cook until cheese melts, about 20 seconds more.

4   Place a burger on bottom buns. Top with desired toppings, then close with top buns.

AVOID A STICKY SITUATION

Spray your spatula lightly with cooking spray to make sure the meat doesn't stick to it when smashing your patties.

SHALLOW FRYING

Also called pan frying, this cooking method uses sizzling oil to get food extra crispy (and therefore extra delicious).

It's important to use caution while working with hot oil, and we recommend using a heavy-bottom pan like a cast-iron skillet with sides that are at least 2 inches high. It's also crucial you make sure your pan or skillet is completely dry before adding oil. Otherwise, once the oil heats, it will start to dangerously splatter!

1
Pour in oil. Pour cooking oil into a high-sided, heavy-bottomed skillet or a heavy pot until it is about one inch deep. Heat the oil over medium heat until it shimmers.

2
Fry. Carefully drop food into the oil (be careful of hot oil splatter!) and fry until golden brown. Use tongs or a spider strainer (pictured) to flip, if necessary, according to your recipe.

3
Remove. Use a spider strainer, tongs, or a metal slotted spoon to remove the food from the pan, taking care to let excess oil drip back into the pan. Transfer to a paper towel—lined plate to cool.

4
Cool the oil. Cool the frying oil completely before disposing. Oil should not be poured down the kitchen sink. Once the oil is cold, pour it into a waterproof, sealable bag or other disposable container and throw it away in the trash.

1

TEST OIL HEAT
Sprinkle a pinch of flour into the oil; if it sizzles, the oil is ready. If it does not sizzle, continue to heat the oil before adding ingredients.

3

2

4

You can fry frozen foods without thawing! You may need to cook the ingredients for 1 to 2 minutes longer.

Don't crowd the pan! You've heard this before, but it is key to extra-crispy results.

Be patient. It's hard to resist peeking! Extra flipping will make the process take longer.

Remember the finishing touches. Drain fried food on paper towels and season with salt.

WHAT YOU'LL NEED

- 2 shallow bowls
- Measuring cups
- Whisk
- Large baking sheet
- Parchment paper
- Large pot
- Ruler
- Tongs
- Paper towels
- Plate
- Large serving platter

TOTAL TIME
1 HOUR AND
10 MINUTES

SERVES 6

Toasted Ravioli

It's so much fun to eat ravioli with your hands! Breaded and fried and showered with Parmesan, this cheesy snack originated in the 1940s at an Italian-American restaurant in St. Louis where they're called "t-ravs." Legend has it a chef dropped the pasta into the fryer instead of the boiling water. Oops!

INGREDIENTS

- 2 large eggs
- ½ cup milk
- 1 cup Italian bread crumbs
- ¼ cup finely grated Parmesan, plus more for serving
- Kosher salt
- Freshly ground black pepper
- 1 pound frozen ravioli, (meat, cheese, or spinach)
- Vegetable oil, for frying
- Marinara, warmed, for serving

DIRECTIONS

1 In a shallow bowl, whisk eggs and milk. In another shallow bowl, combine bread crumbs and Parmesan; season with salt and pepper.

2 Working one at a time, dip ravioli into egg mixture, letting excess drip off, then into bread-crumb mixture, pressing to adhere. Arrange on a large parchment-lined baking sheet. Freeze until solid, about 30 minutes.

3 Into a large pot, pour oil to a depth of 2 inches. Heat over medium heat until shimmering. Working in batches, fry ravioli, turning with tongs, until golden brown and pasta is cooked through, 3 to 4 minutes. Transfer to a paper towel-lined plate; immediately sprinkle with more Parmesan.

4 Transfer ravioli to a platter. Serve warm with marinara alongside for dipping.

BREADING BASICS

If you use the same hand to dip ravioli into the egg mixture and then the bread-crumb mixture, your fingertips will get coated in a sticky, clumpy mess. Instead, use one hand to dip in the egg mixture, and reserve the other hand for only touching the dry bread crumbs.

WHAT YOU'LL NEED

- Box grater
- Cheesecloth or clean dish towel
- Large mixing bowl
- Measuring spoons and cups
- Wooden spoon
- Large skillet
- Spatula
- Small mixing bowl
- Spoon
- Large serving platter

TOTAL TIME
45 MINUTES

SERVES 4

Parmesan Zucchini Fritters

We're starting to put all the skills together: Use a box grater to prep the zucchini for these fritters and then practice shallow frying until they are golden brown and delicious.

INGREDIENTS

- 1   pound zucchini (about 2 large)
- ½   yellow onion, finely chopped
- 3   large eggs, beaten to blend
- ½   teaspoon garlic powder
-    Kosher salt
-    Freshly ground black pepper
- ¾   cup (90 grams) all-purpose flour
- ½   cup finely grated Parmesan
- 2   tablespoons extra-virgin olive oil
- ½   cup marinara
- 1   clove garlic, finely chopped
- 1   tablespoon thinly sliced fresh basil
- 1   teaspoon crushed red pepper flakes (optional)

DIRECTIONS

1. On the large holes of a box grater, grate zucchini. Using a cheesecloth or clean dish towel, squeeze out as much liquid as possible. Transfer zucchini to a large bowl. Add onion, eggs, and garlic powder; season with salt and black pepper and stir to combine. Mix in flour and Parmesan and stir until fully incorporated.

3. In a large skillet over medium–high heat, heat oil. Scoop ¼ cup batter per fritter into skillet and cook, turning halfway through, until golden brown, about 2 minutes per side.

4. In a small bowl, combine marinara, garlic, basil, and red pepper flakes (if using).

5. Transfer fritters to a platter. Serve with sauce alongside.

LESS WATER = MORE CRISP

Zucchini is packed with water. If you keep all that moisture in the batter, the fritters will steam when they hit the hot oil. This will make your fritters soggy. Squeezing out the extra liquid after grating the zucchini ensures the crispiest fritters.

LEVEL 4

Toasting

CINNAMON TOAST + BEST-EVER GRANOLA

P. 124

Broiling

CHICKEN PARMESAN + S'MORES BROWNIES

P. 130

Kneading

CALZONES + CINNAMON SUGAR PRETZEL NUGGETS

P. 136

Creaming

SUGAR COOKIE FRIES + HOSTESS SHEET CAKE

P. 142

TOASTING

You can toast dry ingredients on the stovetop or in the oven. Always watch food closely while toasting, as it can burn quickly.

HOW TO TOAST IN A OVEN

1

Arrange ingredients in single layer. Place ingredients on a dry rimmed baking sheet and arrange them in an even single layer. Heat oven according to your recipe.

2

Toast. Bake, stirring or flipping occasionally, until ingredients are browned and fragrant.

3

Transfer. Use oven mitts or clean kitchen towel to remove baking sheet from oven and immediately transfer toasted items to a plate, parchment, or tray to cool. If you leave them on the hot baking sheet, they will continue to toast and even start to burn.

1

2

HOW TO TOAST ON A STOVETOP

1

Arrange ingredients in a single layer. Place ingredients in a dry skillet and spread in an even layer.

2

Heat. Heat the pan over medium heat.

3

Toast. Using a wooden spoon or rubber spatula, stir or toss ingredients frequently to make sure everything toasts evenly. Continue to toast until ingredients are browned and fragrant.

4

Transfer. Transfer toasted items to a plate or tray to cool. If you leave them in the hot skillet, they will continue to toast and even start to burn.

WHAT YOU'LL NEED

- o Foil
- o Baking sheet
- o Oven mitts
- o Tongs
- o Small bowl
- o Measuring spoons
- o Whisk
- o Butter knife
- o Plates

TOTAL TIME
15 MINUTES

SERVES 4

Cinnamon Toast

This comforting snack is one our favorites from when we were kids just like you! It's super simple: Toast the bread so it's crisp but still tender in the center and then slather it with butter and generously sprinkle with cinnamon sugar.

INGREDIENTS

- 4 thick slices bread, such as white, whole wheat, or cinnamon raisin
- 2 tablespoons granulated sugar
- 1½ teaspoons ground cinnamon
- Pinch of kosher salt
- 4 tablespoons unsalted butter, room temperature

DIRECTIONS

1 Preheat oven to 350°F. Arrange bread on a foil-lined baking sheet. Bake, turning halfway through, until toasted and light golden, 10 to 12 minutes.

2 Meanwhile, in a small bowl, combine sugar, cinnamon, and salt.

3 Divide toast among plates. Spread butter on top side of each toast. Generously sprinkle with cinnamon sugar.

MIX IT UP!
Take your toast to the next level by adding banana slices or substituting the butter with peanut butter or hazelnut spread. Feeling warm and cozy? Mix the cinnamon and sugar with some pumpkin pie or apple pie spice.

WHAT YOU'LL NEED

- o 18-inch-by-13-inch sheet tray
- o Parchment paper
- o Large mixing bowl
- o Measuring cups and spoons
- o Rubber spatula
- o Oven mitts
- o Airtight container, if storing

HOW TO STORE

Keep your granola in an airtight container or zip-top bag in a cool place on a counter or in a cabinet. It'll keep for up to 2 weeks (if it lasts that long!).

TOTAL TIME
1 HOUR

MAKES 5 CUPS

Best-Ever Granola

This homemade granola—the perfect combination of sweet, savory, crunchy, and chewy—is incredibly customizable and 100 percent better than its store-bought alternative. Enjoy it sprinkled over a bowl of yogurt with fresh berries or by the handful.

INGREDIENTS

- 2⅓ cups old-fashioned oats
- ⅔ cup unsweetened coconut flakes
- ⅓ cup chopped raw pecans
- ⅓ cup chopped walnuts
- ¼ cup (55 grams) packed light brown sugar
- ¼ cup extra-virgin olive oil
- ¼ cup pure maple syrup
- ½ teaspoon kosher salt
- ½ teaspoon pure vanilla extract
- ¼ teaspoon ground cinnamon
- ¼ cup dried apricots
- ¼ cup packed raisins

DIRECTIONS

1. Preheat oven to 300°F. Line an 18-inch-by-13-inch sheet tray with parchment. In a large bowl, toss oats, coconut, pecans, walnuts, brown sugar, oil, syrup, salt, vanilla, and cinnamon. Pour mixture onto prepared tray and pack to an 11-inch-by-9-inch rectangle.

2. Bake granola 15 minutes. Use oven mitts to remove from oven and stir to break up mixture. Compact back to a rectangle with a spatula and continue to bake until lightly golden brown, about 30 minutes more. Give it another toss if color is still slightly under golden brown and continue to bake in 3- to 5-minute increments; the edges will start to darken more quickly. Let cool 10 minutes.

3. Break up into small clusters. Gently fold in apricots and raisins, then let cool completely.

SWITCH IT UP

Create your own ideal granola by mixing up these ingredients.

OIL

Olive oil helps keep this snack from being too sweet, but you could also use coconut oil or avocado oil.

NUTS OR SEEDS

Swap in alternatives like almonds or pepitas, or omit entirely if you or anyone in your house has allergies. Make sure nuts or seeds are raw and untoasted for this recipe.

FRUIT

You could swap in any dried fruit you like. It's best to toss the dried fruit into the granola after it's been baked so that it doesn't turn into burnt fruit.

BROILING

Broiling is like upside-down grilling! This cooking method uses direct heat to add color and crispiness to food. But watch out: The intensity of the broiler's heat can turn food from pleasantly browned to scorched in seconds!

1

Prepare. Arrange an oven rack 4 to 6 inches under the broiler.

2

Turn on broiler. Turn the broiler on high and wait a few minutes for it to heat up.

3

Slide food under broiler. Place ingredients on a rimmed baking sheet and carefully slide the sheet onto the oven rack under the broiler.

4

Remove. Once food is browned or crisped as specified by your recipe, remove the tray from under the broiler.

It's important to wear oven mitts when you are using an oven to cook (including broiling!).

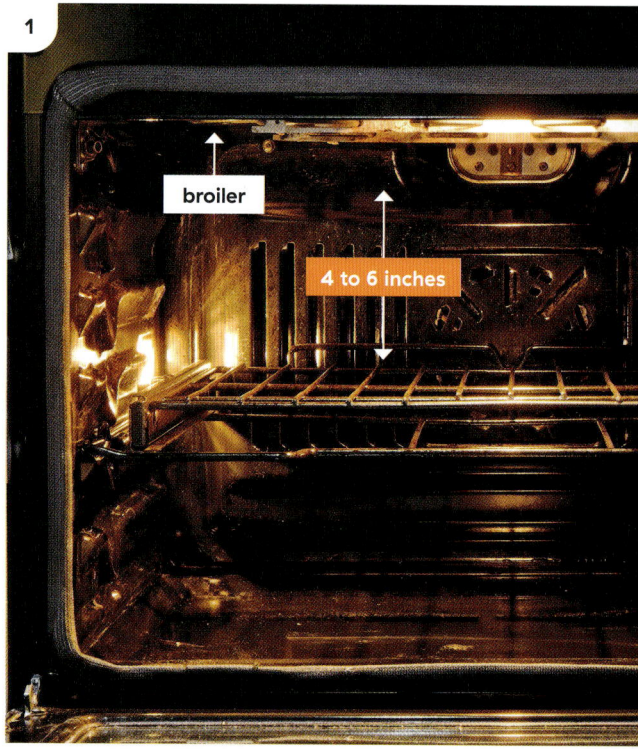

1

broiler

4 to 6 inches

3

2

4

WHAT YOU'LL NEED

- o Box grater
- o 3 shallow bowls
- o Measuring cups and spoons
- o Fork
- o Paper towels
- o Small mixing bowl
- o Large pot
- o Deep-fry or instant-read thermometer
- o Wire rack
- o Rimmed baking sheet
- o Tongs
- o Spoon
- o Oven mitts
- o Plates

TOTAL TIME
1 HOUR

SERVES 6

Chicken Parmesan

This classic recipe has everything you want, full stop: a fried crispy chicken cutlets, a perfect blend of mozzarella and Parm, and a sauce full of flavor with herby basil and a hint of sweetness.

INGREDIENTS

- 1 cup panko bread crumbs
- 1 teaspoon garlic powder
- 2 cups finely grated Parmesan, divided
- ¾ cup (90 grams) all-purpose flour
- 2 large eggs
- 6 (¼-inch-thick) boneless, skinless chicken cutlets (about 1½ pounds total)
- Kosher salt
- Freshly ground black pepper
- 1 cup shredded mozzarella
- 1 cup vegetable or canola oil
- 1 (24-ounce) jar marinara
- Chopped fresh basil, for serving

DIRECTIONS

1 In a shallow bowl, combine panko, garlic powder, and 1 cup Parmesan. Into another shallow bowl, pour flour. In a third shallow bowl, beat eggs with 1 tablespoon water.

2 Pat chicken dry; season with salt and pepper. Dip chicken into flour, shaking off excess, then into egg, then into panko mixture, gently pressing to adhere.

3 In a small bowl, mix mozzarella and remaining 1 cup Parmesan.

4 In a large, heavy pot over medium heat, heat oil until a deep-fry or instant-read thermometer registers 350°F; if it smokes a bit, that's okay. Set a wire rack in a rimmed baking sheet.

5 Working one at a time and with an adult, fry chicken until one side is golden brown, about 1 minute. Flip and continue to fry until golden brown on the other side and the sound of the frying chicken gets slightly louder—this is the moisture evaporating from the chicken—about 1 minute more. Transfer to prepared rack. Repeat with remaining chicken. Spoon some marinara over chicken. Sprinkle with cheese mixture.

6 Turn on broiler. Broil, watching closely, until cheese is melted and brown spots form, about 2 minutes.

7 Divide chicken among plates. Top with basil. Serve with remaining marinara alongside.

WHAT'S THE BEST WAY TO BREAD CHICKEN?

To avoid ending this process with hands that look just like your chicken cutlets, it's best to have a "dry" hand for dry ingredient and a "wet" hand for wet ingredients while breading cutlets.

- 9-inch-by-9-inch baking pan

- Large bowl

- Measuring cups

- Rubber spatula

- Cake tester or wooden skewer

- Oven mitts

- Chef's knife

- Plates

TOTAL TIME
1 HOUR AND
5 MINUTES

SERVES 16

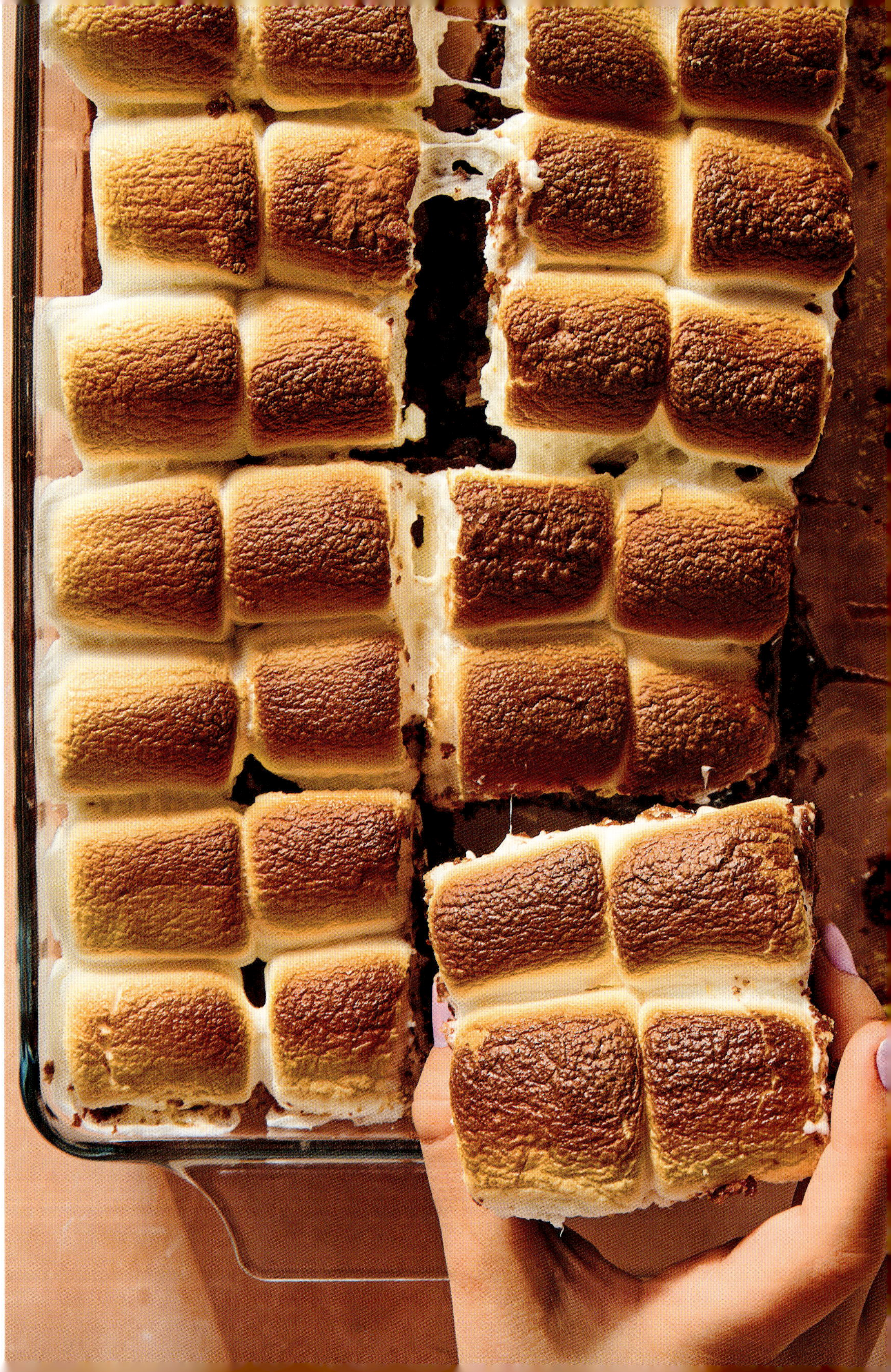

USE YOUR SKILL

S'mores Brownies

Gooey, fudgy brownies topped with broiled marshmallows remind us of campfire s'mores—just even better.

INGREDIENTS

Cooking spray
6   graham crackers
1   box brownie mix, plus ingredients called for on box
1   cup chopped Hershey's chocolate bars
1   (10-ounce) bag marshmallows

DIRECTIONS

1   Place a rack in upper third of oven; preheat to 350°F. Spray a 9-inch-by-9-inch baking pan with cooking spray. Layer bottom of pan with graham crackers, trimming crackers to cover bottom of pan in a single layer.

2   Prepare brownies mix according to box directions. Fold chopped Hershey's bars into brownies batter. Pour batter over crackers and spread in an even layer.

3   Bake brownies until a tester inserted into the center comes out clean, 30 to 35 minutes.

4   Use oven mitts to remove baking pan from oven and turn broiler on high. Arrange marshmallows in an even layer on top of brownies.

5   Broil brownies, watching closely as the marshmallows will go from golden brown to burnt quickly, and remove as soon as marshmallows turn golden brown, 1 to 3 minutes.

6   Let cool at least 15 minutes or let cool completely. Using a knife sprayed with cooking spray, slice brownies into pieces.

MARSHMALLOW COOKING TIME
Get the perfect doneness every single time.

2 MIN
Lightly toasted golden exterior, no gooey interior

3 MIN
Crisp deep, golden brown exterior, slightly gooey interior

4 MIN
Slightly charred, evenly brown exterior, melty and gooey interior

KNEADING

Working the dough this way forms a smooth, cohesive dough and creates gluten strands, which give dough, and thus baked goods, their chewiness and overall structure.

1–2
Flour surface. Sprinkle flour on your work surface and place a ball of dough on the floured surface.

3–4
Push. Use the heel of your hand to push the dough down and away from you.

5–6
Rotate. Rotate the dough around slightly, about 45 degrees.

7–8
Fold. Use your fingers to scoop up the pushed dough and fold it over itself.

9
Repeat. Continue to push, fold, and rotate until the dough becomes smooth and springy.

DOUGH HOOK

TOOLBOX

DOUGH HOOK

Using a stand mixer with a dough hook can cut the time it takes to knead dough in half compared to manual kneading.

WHAT YOU'LL NEED

- ○ Large mixing bowl
- ○ Measuring cups and spoons
- ○ Whisk
- ○ Medium mixing bowl
- ○ Wooden spoon
- ○ Plastic wrap
- ○ 2 large baking sheets
- ○ Bench scraper or knife
- ○ Rolling pin
- ○ Ruler
- ○ Spoons
- ○ Pastry brush
- ○ Kitchen scissors or paring knife
- ○ Oven mitts

TOTAL TIME
1 HOUR AND 10 MINUTES, PLUS DOUGH RISING TIME

SERVES 4

For a shortcut use store-bought pizza dough, either fresh from the store or a pizzeria or from a can.

Calzones

Calzones are like an individual pizza all wrapped up, which means no cheese sliding off, no floppy crusts, and it's completely portable. Pure deliciousness wrapped up in a pillowy dough—we'll take a calzone any day.

INGREDIENTS

FOR THE DOUGH

1 tablespoon kosher salt

3⅓ cups (400 grams) plus ¼ cup (30 grams) bread flour, divided, plus more for dusting

1⅓ cups lukewarm water (about 100°F)

4 teaspoons honey

1 (¼-ounce) packet active dry yeast

FOR THE CALZONES

Cooking spray

All-purpose flour, for surface

1 cup pizza sauce

1 cup ricotta

½ cup pepperoni

1 cup shredded mozzarella

Extra-virgin olive oil, for brushing

Kosher salt

DIRECTIONS

1 **Prepare the dough** In a large, deep bowl, whisk salt and 3⅓ cups flour. In a medium bowl, mix water, honey, yeast, until yeast just about dissolves. Pour honey mixture into dry ingredients. Using your hands, push mixture together to form a cohesive dough. Turn out onto a clean surface and knead with 3 to 4 tablespoons flour until smooth, 1 to 2 minutes.

2 Transfer dough to a lightly floured bowl and cover with plastic wrap (this can be the same bowl you made the dough in). Let sit at room temperature at least 12 hours, up to 18. If resting goes beyond 18 hours, refrigerate and bring to room temperature before baking.

3 Press down on dough to deflate. Turn out onto a clean work surface. Form into a loose ball, then fold dough in on itself from beneath, about 8 times. The dough should be in a tight ball at this point. Let rest 10 to 15 minutes.

4 **Assemble the calzones** Preheat oven to 500°F and grease 2 large baking sheets with cooking spray. Divide 1¾ pounds dough into 4 pieces; reserve remaining dough for another use. On a lightly floured surface, roll one piece of dough to an 8-inch circle, about ¼ inch thick. Spoon one-quarter of pizza sauce in middle of dough, then dot with one-quarter of ricotta. Top with one-quarter of pepperoni and one-quarter of mozzarella.

5 Gently fold dough in half, dampen seams with water, and pinch together, then crimp edges all around. Repeat with remaining dough. Transfer to prepared baking sheets. Brush tops with oil and sprinkle with salt. Using kitchen scissors or a paring knife, slit tops in 2 to 3 spots to create steam vents.

6 Bake calzones, brushing with oil and rotating sheets top to bottom halfway through, until tops are golden brown and filling is bubbling, about 20 minutes. Let cool 5 minutes before cutting open.

WHAT YOU'LL NEED

- 2 medium mixing bowls

- Measuring cups and spoons

- Whisk

- 3 large mixing bowls

- Rubber spatula

- Plastic wrap

- Baking sheets

- Parchment paper

- Bench scraper or paring knife

- Large pot

- Slotted spoon or spider strainer

TOTAL TIME
2 HOURS

MAKES 48

CREAM CHEESE FROSTING

Pour 2 tablespoons melted unsalted butter into a large bowl. In a medium bowl, whisk ⅓ cup granulated sugar, 4 teaspoons ground cinnamon, and a large pinch of kosher salt until combined. In another medium bowl, whisk 1 cup confectioners' sugar, 2 ounces cream cheese, and 2 tablespoons whole milk until smooth. Drizzle frosting on top or serve on the side for dipping.

USE YOUR SKILL

Cinnamon Sugar Pretzel Nuggets

Is it even possible to walk by a pretzel store and not be drawn in by the smell of cinnamon-sugary pretzel bites? Once the aroma fills the air, we suddenly need a bucket, ASAP.

INGREDIENTS

FOR THE PRETZELS

¾ cup warm water (between 110°F and 115°F)

1 teaspoon granulated sugar

1¼ teaspoons active dry yeast

2¼ cups (270 grams) all-purpose flour, plus more for surface

Kosher salt

Cooking spray

½ cup baking soda

FOR THE COATING

3 tablespoons unsalted butter, melted

⅓ cup (67 grams) granulated sugar

4 teaspoons ground cinnamon

Kosher salt

DIRECTIONS

1 **Make the pretzels** In a medium bowl, stir warm water and granulated sugar until sugar is dissolved. Sprinkle yeast over. Let sit until yeast begins to foam and bubble, about 5 minutes.

2 In a large bowl, whisk flour and ¾ teaspoon salt to combine. Scrape yeast mixture into dry ingredients and stir until a shaggy dough forms. Scrape dough onto a clean work surface and knead until dough is smooth, about 5 minutes.

3 Spray another large bowl with cooking spray. Place dough in bowl, cover with plastic, and let sit in a warm spot until doubled in size, 1 hour to 1 hour and 30 minutes.

4 Preheat oven to 450°F. Line a baking sheet with parchment and spray with cooking spray. On a lightly floured surface, divide dough into 4 pieces. Working one at a time and keeping the other pieces covered with plastic, roll dough into a 12-inch-long rope, ½ to ¾ inch thick. Cut rope into 1-inch-wide nuggets. Gently roll each nugget on work surface to even out the shape. Arrange on prepared sheet. Repeat with remaining dough.

5 Bring a large pot of water to a boil. Stir in baking soda and return to a boil. Cook nuggets, tossing a few times, until light golden brown and just cooked through, about 30 seconds. Using a slotted spoon or spider strainer, scoop out nuggets, leaving excess water in pot, and return to baking sheet.

6 Bake pretzel nuggets until deep golden brown, 12 to 15 minutes.

7 **Make the coating** Pour butter into a large bowl. In a medium bowl, whisk granulated sugar, cinnamon, and a large pinch of salt until combined.

8 Immediately transfer pretzels to butter and toss to combine. Working in batches, toss butter-coated pretzels in cinnamon sugar until coated.

CREAMING

Blending butter and sugar together until it's light and fluffy is called "creaming." You can use a wooden spoon and blend the ingredients together by hand, but it will take quite a long time—and a lot of muscle!

HOW TO CREAM WITH A STAND MIXER

1

Use room–temperature ingredients. Place room–temperature butter and sugar in the bowl of a stand mixer fitted with the paddle attachment.

2–3

Beat them together. Beat on medium–high speed until pale in color and fluffy, about 5 minutes.

1

2

ADDING AIR IS A TEXTURE GAME-CHANGER

Mixing at a high speed for a long time brings air bubbles into the ingredients. These bubbles get trapped in the butter and form pockets of air that make the mixture fluffy. The sugar dissolves in the water from the butter, making everything smooth instead of gritty (like the original granules of sugar before creaming).

3

HOW TO CREAM WITH A HANDHELD MIXER

1

Use room-temperature ingredients. Place room-temperature butter and sugar in a mixing bowl.

2

Beat them together. Use a handheld electric mixer to beat the mixture until it is pale in color and fluffy, 6 to 8 minutes.

WHAT YOU'LL NEED

- Stand mixer with whisk attachment
- Measuring cups and spoons
- Rubber spatula
- Plastic wrap
- Rolling pin
- 2 large baking sheets
- Parchment paper
- Pizza wheel or knife
- Oven mitts
- Large serving platter

TOTAL TIME
1 HOUR, PLUS CHILLING TIME

SERVES 12

USE YOUR SKILL

Sugar Cookie Fries

Fries that taste like sugar cookies and are the best kind. You can also serve them with birthday cake frosting, hazelnut–cocoa spread, or strawberry jam.

INGREDIENTS

1   cup (2 sticks) unsalted butter, softened

1   cup (200 grams) granulated sugar, plus more for sprinkling

1   large egg

2   teaspoons pure vanilla extract

3   cups (360 grams) all-purpose flour, plus more for surface

¾   teaspoon baking powder

½   teaspoon kosher salt

    Funfetti frosting, strawberry jam, and Nutella, for serving

DIRECTIONS

1   In the large bowl of a stand mixer fitted with the whisk attachment, beat butter and sugar on medium speed until light and fluffy, about 2 minutes. Add egg and beat until combined. Beat in vanilla. Add flour, baking powder, and salt and beat on low speed until just combined.

2   Divide dough into 2 balls and flatten into discs. Wrap discs with plastic wrap and refrigerate for 1 hour.

3   Roll out 1 dough disc by following directions at right.

4   Sprinkle with sugar and transfer dough to 2 parchment–lined baking sheets. Repeat with second disc. Refrigerate until cold, about 1 hour.

5   Preheat oven to 350°F.

6   Bake cookie fries until starting to turn golden around the edges, 12 to 15 minutes.

7   Transfer cookie fries to a platter. Serve with desired dipping sauces alongside.

HOW TO CUT FRIES

1
Roll dough disc into a rectangle about ¼ inch thick. (Don't worry if it doesn't have perfect, sharp corners).

2
Cut dough crosswise into ¾–inch strips

3
Cut the strips in half.

4
Use a knife or a pizza cutter to trim the edges to make straight sides.

WHAT YOU'LL NEED

- 12-inch-by-17-inch half sheet or jelly roll pan
- Large mixing bowl
- Measuring cups and spoons
- Wooden spoon
- Rubber spatula
- Cake tester or wooden skewer
- Wire rack
- Stand mixer with whisk attachment
- Offset spatula
- Medium heatproof bowl
- Small saucepan
- Whisk
- Medium mixing bowl
- Spoon
- Pastry bag
- Small piping tip

TOTAL TIME
1 HOUR

SERVES 10 TO 12

To make this cake look just like the famous Hostess cupcakes, pipe a decorative doodle pattern on a diagonal across the ganache.

USE YOUR SKILL

Hostess Sheet Cake

Fudgy, cream-filled cupcakes have been an American treasure
for over 100 years. To really complete the copycat
Hostess-inspired look, pipe icing in the traditional, iconic loops.
(You'll have to skip ahead to piping skills on page 180!)

INGREDIENTS

Cooking spray

All-purpose flour,
for pan

1   (15.25-ounce) box
    devil's food cake
    mix, plus ingredients
    called for on box

2   (7.5-ounce) jars
    Marshmallow Fluff

1   cup (2 sticks)
    unsalted butter,
    softened

2   teaspoons kosher
    salt

2   teaspoons pure
    vanilla extract

3   cups (345 grams)
    (or more)
    confectioners' sugar,
    divided

1½ cups semisweet
    chocolate chips

¾   cup heavy cream

1   tablespoon (or more)
    whole milk

DIRECTIONS

1   Preheat oven to 350°F. Generously grease a 17-inch-
    by-12-inch half-sheet or jelly roll pan with cooking
    spray; lightly sprinkle with flour, tapping out excess.

2   In a large bowl, prepare cake batter according to box
    directions. Spread batter into prepared pan; smooth
    into a thin, even layer with a rubber spatula.

3   Bake cake until a cake tester inserted into the center
    comes out clean, 22 to 25 minutes. Let cool in pan on
    a wire rack.

4   Meanwhile, in the large bowl of a stand mixer fitted
    with the whisk attachment, beat Fluff and butter
    until smooth and fluffy. Add salt, vanilla, and 2 cups
    confectioners' sugar and beat until smooth.

5   Using an offset spatula, spread marshmallow frosting
    on cooled cake.

6   Place chocolate chips in a medium heatproof bowl.
    In a small saucepan over medium heat, heat cream
    until bubbles begin to break the surface around
    edges of pan. Pour hot cream over chips, swirling
    bowl to coat chips. Cover bowl and let sit 3 to
    5 minutes. Uncover and, starting from the center
    and working your way to edges of bowl, gently
    whisk until chocolate is melted and smooth.
    Let cool to room temperature.

7   Pour cooled chocolate ganache over marshmallow
    frosting; spread with offset spatula. Refrigerate until
    set, about 10 minutes.

8   In a medium bowl, whisk milk and 1 cup confectioners'
    sugar until smooth. If icing is too loose, add more
    confectioners' sugar; if it's too thick, add more milk.

9   Transfer icing to a pastry bag fitted with a small tip.
    Pipe decorative doodle patterns on a diagonal across
    ganache.

LEVEL 5

ROLLING

Rolling dough to the same thickness means cookies, pies, and other baked goods will cook evenly. But the first step is always a generous dusting of flour to avoid sticking!

1

Dust with flour. Sprinkle a small amount of flour (or other dry powder, according to your recipe) evenly over a clean counter so your dough won't stick. Place your dough on the dusted counter. Sprinkle a small amount of flour (or other dry powder, according to your recipe) over the dough.

2

Press and roll. Press a rolling pin down on the surface of the dough and roll it away from your body to slightly flatten the dough.

3–4

Rotate dough. Pick up the dough, check to make sure the counter is still dusted (sprinkle a little more if necessary), and rotate dough 90 degrees.

5–6

Repeat. Repeat rolling, lifting, and rotating until the dough meets the measurement specified in your recipe. Use long, smooth rolling motions.

3

6

LET IT ROLL

There are many types of dough, and the way you roll them varies.

PIZZA DOUGH

A springy dough, like pizza dough, requires time. While it rests, the gluten relaxes and makes the dough easier to stretch.

PIE DOUGH

A buttery dough, like pie dough, is temperature-sensitive and needs to be rolled out relatively quickly to avoid softening.

If the rolling pin begins to stick to the dough, sprinkle more flour (or other dry powder, according to your recipe) over the dough before continuing to roll.

WHAT YOU'LL NEED

- Measuring cups and spoons
- Rolling pin
- Ruler
- Large baking sheet
- Fork
- Pastry brush
- Butter knife or offset spatula

TOTAL TIME
45 MINUTES

SERVES 8

Chocolate Pizza

This dessert pizza is totally customizable. Add some sliced strawberries, marshmallows, pretzels, or candy or just leave it at Nutella! You absolutely can't go wrong.

INGREDIENTS

- 3 tablespoons granulated sugar, divided
- 8 ounces store-bought pizza dough
- 2 tablespoons unsalted butter, melted
- ½ cup Nutella

  Pretzels, marshmallows, sprinkles, and M&M's, for topping

DIRECTIONS

1 Preheat oven to 450°F. Sprinkle about half of sugar onto a clean surface. Place pizza dough on sugar and sprinkle remaining sugar on top. Roll pizza dough out into an 11-inch circle.

2 Transfer dough to a large baking sheet and poke all over with a fork, then brush with melted butter. Bake crust until golden, 12 to 15 minutes. Let cool slightly.

3 Spread Nutella all over crust, leaving a 1-inch border around the edge. Top with pretzels, marshmallows, sprinkles, and M&M's.

SUPER SWEET

Rolling the crust out in sugar prevents it from sticking to the surface. The sugar also caramelizes in the oven and makes the crust extra-good.

WHAT YOU'LL NEED

- o Measuring spoons and cups
- o 2 large mixing bowls
- o Wooden spoon
- o Plastic wrap
- o Rolling pin
- o Pie plate
- o Pastry brush
- o Small mixing bowl
- o Fork
- o Parchment paper or aluminum foil
- o Pie weights or dried beans
- o Handheld mixer
- o Medium mixing bowl
- o Whisk
- o Rubber spatula

TOTAL TIME
30 MINUTES, PLUS CHILLING TIME

SERVES 8 TO 10

Birthday Cake Pie

Imagine the joy of birthday cake and the comfort of pie merging into one whimsical creation that is perfect for any celebration. Enter this fun dessert.

INGREDIENTS

FOR THE CRUST

- 1½ cups (180 grams) all-purpose flour, plus more for rolling
- 2 teaspoons granulated sugar
- ½ teaspoon kosher salt
- ½ cup (1 stick) unsalted butter, thinly chopped
- 3-4 tablespoons ice water
- 3 tablespoons rainbow sprinkles
- 1 large egg, beaten with 1 tablespoon water

FOR THE FILLING

- 1½ cups cold milk
- 1 (3.4-ounce) package instant vanilla pudding mix
- 2 cups heavy cream
- 1 cup vanilla cake mix
- 3 tablespoons rainbow sprinkles, plus more for decorating

DIRECTIONS

1 **Make the crust** In a large bowl, whisk flour, sugar, and salt. Add butter and, using your fingertips, mix into dry ingredients until crumbly. Gradually add 3 to 4 tablespoons ice water, 1 tablespoon at a time, until a pliable dough forms. Fold sprinkles into dough until just combined.

2 On a lightly floured surface, turn out dough and form into a disc. Wrap with plastic wrap and refrigerate at least 1 hour or up to overnight.

3 Preheat oven to 425°F. On a lightly floured surface, roll out dough to a ¼-inch-thick round. Carefully roll dough around rolling pin, then unfurl into a 9-inch pie dish. Trim, leaving about a 1-inch overhang, and crimp edges, if desired. Brush with beaten egg. Line dough with parchment or foil, leaving some overhang. Fill with pie weights or dried beans.

4 Bake crust for 12 minutes. Remove parchment and weights and continue to bake until golden brown, about 5 minutes more. Let cool.

5 **Make the filling** In a medium bowl, whisk milk and pudding mix until combined. Let stand until thickened, about 5 minutes.

6 Meanwhile, in a large bowl, using a handheld mixer on medium-high speed, beat cream until soft peaks form, about 2 minutes. Beat in cake mix until stiff peaks form, about 2 minutes.

7 Add pudding mixture and sprinkles to cream mixture and fold until combined.

8 Pour filling into cooled crust. Sprinkle all over with more sprinkles. Refrigerate until firm, at least 5 hours or up to 1 day.

FROSTING

A smooth, creamy frosting makes any cake or cookie that much sweeter. You can change up the color, flavor, and texture when you know how to make the stuff from scratch.

1

Scoop. Use a butter knife, rubber spatula, or offset spatula to scoop up a small dollop of frosting and plop it on your fully cooled baked good.

2

Spread. Spread frosting using smooth, even strokes. Repeat.

Make sure your frosting is room temperature before you start. If it's too cold, the frosting won't spread smoothly. If it's too warm, it will start to melt.

1

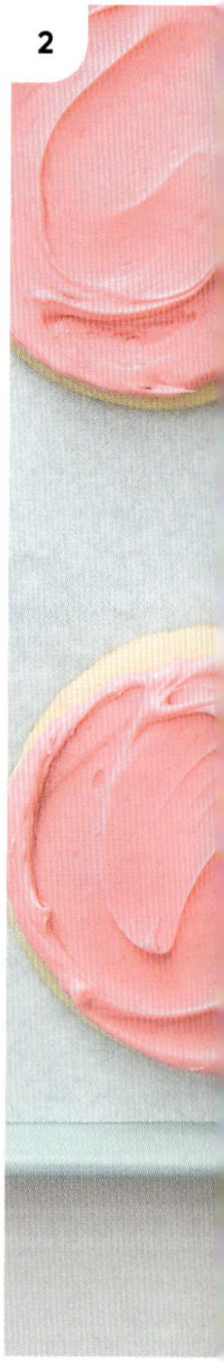

2

RUBBER STRAIGHT OFFSET

TOOLBOX

SPATULAS

Spatulas are essential for spreading. The handy flexible rubber spatula, which helps scrape, fold, and stir is most likely already part of your kitchen tool collection. But you might want to get to know the rubber spatula's rigid cousins. Meet the straight and offset spatulas. They are both perfect for spreading frosting. They come in different sizes for all your baking projects.

LET'S DECORATE!

Once you've mastered spreading frosting in an even, smooth layer, try adding a little texture. Drag the tongs of a fork through smooth frosting to make lines. Use the back of a spoon to make swirls. Draw a zigzag pattern with a toothpick or make your own pattern. Or just add sprinkles!

WHAT YOU'LL NEED

- 3 large mixing bowls
- Measuring cups and spoons
- Whisk
- Handheld electric mixer
- Plastic wrap
- 2 large baking sheets
- Parchment paper
- Rolling pin
- Oven mitts
- 3–inch round cookie cutter
- Offset spatula

Dye the buttercream any color you like and top the frosting with different sprinkles depending on the season (just like the grocery store bakery would do!).

TOTAL TIME
2 HOURS AND 30 MINUTES

MAKES 15

Lofthouse Cookies

You know those thick, soft sugar cookies from the grocery store that had an even thicker layer of frosting on top? These are the homemade version inspired by them and just as good.

INGREDIENTS

FOR THE COOKIES

2¼ cups (270 grams) all-purpose flour, plus more for surface

¼ cup cornstarch

1 teaspoon baking powder

1 teaspoon kosher salt

1 cup (200 grams) granulated sugar

½ cup (1 stick) unsalted butter, softened

4 ounces cream cheese, softened

1 large egg

1 teaspoon pure vanilla extract

½ teaspoon almond extract

FOR THE BUTTERCREAM

¾ cup (1½ sticks) unsalted butter, softened

2¾ cups (315 grams) confectioners' sugar

1 tablespoon heavy cream

1 teaspoon pure vanilla extract

Pinch of kosher salt

Food coloring

Sprinkles, for decorating

DIRECTIONS

1 **Make the cookies** In a large bowl, whisk flour, cornstarch, baking powder, and salt.

2 In another large bowl, using a handheld mixer on medium–high speed, beat granulated sugar, butter, and cream cheese until light and fluffy, about 3 minutes. Add egg, vanilla extract, and almond extract and beat until well combined. Add dry ingredients and beat on medium–low speed until just combined.

3 Place dough on a sheet of plastic wrap and smooth into a disc; the dough will still be soft and sticky at this point. Refrigerate until well chilled, at least 1 hour or up to 8.

4 Preheat oven to 350°F. On a lightly floured work surface, turn out dough. Dust top of dough with flour, then roll to ½ inch thick. Using a 3-inch round cookie cutter, cut out rounds and arrange on 2 large parchment–lined baking sheets, spacing 2 inches apart. Gather scraps and reroll to cut out more rounds.

5 Bake cookies until edges are just set but centers are still slightly underdone (they shouldn't gain much color on top), 10 to 12 minutes. Let cool on sheets.

6 **Make the frosting** In a large bowl, using handheld mixer on medium–high speed, beat butter until smooth and creamy, about 2 minutes. Add confectioners' sugar and continue to beat until light and fluffy, about 3 minutes more. Add cream, vanilla, and salt and beat until combined. Add desired food coloring and beat to combine.

7 Using an offset spatula, frost tops of cookies with a thick amount of frosting. Top with sprinkles.

WHAT YOU'LL NEED

- o 8-inch-by-8-inch baking pan
- o Parchment paper
- o Large mixing bowl
- o Whisk
- o Rubber spatula
- o Measuring cups
- o Offset spatula or spoon
- o Oven mitts
- o Aluminum foil
- o Cake tester or wooden skewer
- o Wire cooling rack
- o Medium mixing bowl
- o Measuring spoons
- o Chef's knife or serrated knife
- o Cutting board

TOTAL TIME
1 HOUR AND 45 MINUTES, PLUS RESTING TIME

SERVES 12

USE YOUR SKILL

Strawberry Pop-Tart Blondies

Buttery, chewy, and filled with strawberry jam, this toaster pastry–inspired bar cookie is pure bliss. Strawberry jam is a classic, but you can mix it up with other flavors.

INGREDIENTS

Cooking spray

1¼ cups (270 grams) packed light brown sugar

¾ cup (1½ sticks) unsalted butter, melted

¼ cup (50 grams) granulated sugar

2 large eggs

2 teaspoons pure vanilla extract

½ teaspoon kosher salt

2 cups (240 grams) all-purpose flour

1 cup strawberry jam

1 cup (115 grams) confectioners' sugar

1-2 tablespoons whole milk

Sprinkles, for decorating

CLEAN CUT

A chef's knife will work just fine for cutting these bars, but a serrated knife will give you a cleaner cut.

DIRECTIONS

1 Preheat oven to 350°F. Grease an 8-inch-by-8-inch baking pan with cooking spray and line with parchment, leaving an overhang on 2 opposite sides.

2 In a large bowl, whisk brown sugar, butter, and granulated sugar until well combined. Whisk in eggs, vanilla, and salt. Stir in flour until just combined.

3 Spread 1½ cups batter in bottom of prepared pan. Top with dollops of jam, then gently spread jam over batter with an offset spatula or the back of a spoon.

4 Dollop remaining batter over jam. Using offset spatula or the back of a spoon, gently smooth batter in an even layer, being careful not to disturb jam layer. (The goal is to trap the jam in the middle, like a Pop-Tart.)

5 Bake blondies, tenting with foil if darkening too quickly, until golden around the edges and a cake tester inserted into the center comes out with a few moist crumbs attached, 45 to 50 minutes. Let cool in pan 15 minutes, then lift out of pan using parchment overhang and transfer blondies to a wire rack. Let cool completely.

6 In a medium bowl, whisk confectioners' sugar and 1 tablespoon milk until smooth, adding more milk by the ½ teaspoonful until glaze is thick yet pourable.

7 Pour glaze over cooled blondies and spread with offset spatula. Top with sprinkles. Let glaze rest until set, about 1 hour. Cut into rectangles.

MELTING

To successfully melt ingredients without burning them, use gentle heat and stir often. You can use the microwave or the stovetop.

HOW TO MELT ON STOVETOP

1

Simmer water. Fill a small pot with about 1 inch of water and bring it to a simmer over medium heat.

2

Prepare bowl. Place ingredient(s) in a medium heatproof bowl.

3

Assemble double boiler.
Place the heatproof bowl on top of the simmering pot (be careful as the steam will be hot).

4

Stir. Use a rubber spatula to stir the ingredient (or mixture of ingredients) until it is fully melted.

5

Carefully remove. Lift the bowl from atop the pot when done, keeping in mind that the bottom of the bowl will be hot and wet. Use a clean kitchen towel or oven mitts.

3

5

HOW TO MELT IN MICROWAVE

1
Prepare bowl. Place ingredient(s) in a microwave-safe bowl.

2
Microwave. Microwave on 50 percent power for 30 seconds.

3
Stir. Remove bowl, stir, and return to microwave.

4
Repeat. Repeat microwaving and stirring until ingredient (or mixture of ingredients) is fully melted.

WHAT YOU'LL NEED

- ○ Measuring spoon
- ○ Clean kitchen towel
- ○ 4 ice-pop sticks
- ○ Shallow plates (for toppings)
- ○ Small saucepan
- ○ Wooden spoon or rubber spatula
- ○ Spoon
- ○ Baking sheet
- ○ Parchment paper

TOTAL TIME
30 MINUTES

SERVES 4

Oreos + M&M's

Reese's Peanut Butter Cups + Pretzels

Fruity Pebbles

Marshmallows + graham crackers + chocolate chips

Heath Bar + honey roasted peanuts

Caramel Apples

No need to wait for the county fair to enjoy this classic autumn treat. Make them at home and add your favorite toppings. We love Granny Smith apples for the crunch and tartness, but Honeycrisp, Fuji, or any type of apple you love eating will work too.

INGREDIENTS

4   Granny Smith apples

Toasted chopped peanuts, crushed cereal, sprinkles, and/or chopped Oreos, for topping

1   (11-ounce) bag soft caramels

2   tablespoons water

DIRECTIONS

1   Wash and dry apples. Insert ice-pop sticks 1 to 2 inches into the center of each apple. Place desired toppings on shallow plates.

2   Unwrap caramels and transfer to a small saucepan. Heat over medium-low heat and add water. Cook, stirring frequently with a wooden spoon or rubber spatula, until candy is melted and no lumps are visible, 12 to 15 minutes.

3   Remove saucepan from heat. Working quickly, coat apples in caramel, holding handle of saucepan and tilting it slightly to the side so caramel pools to one side. When you get to the very bottom of the pot, coat apples with a spoon.

4   Dip caramel-covered apples directly into desired toppings. Arrange apples on a parchment-lined baking sheet and refrigerate until ready to serve. Let sit at room temperature 10 to 15 minutes before serving.

Caramel popcorn + M&M's

SLIPPERY CARAMEL

If you're struggling to keep the caramel from sliding down the apple, try chilling the apples in the refrigerator overnight before dipping. The cold surface will harden the caramel faster as you dip the apples. Another common culprit for slippery caramel is moisture on the surface of the apples, so make sure you pat them dry completely before dipping.

WHAT YOU'LL NEED

- 8-inch or 9-inch square pan
- Parchment paper
- Large mixing bowl
- Measuring spoons and cups
- Handheld electric mixer
- Small microwave-safe bowl
- Medium mixing bowl
- Rubber spatula
- Chef's knife
- Cutting board

TOTAL TIME
20 MINUTES, PLUS CHILLING TIME

SERVES 24

USE YOUR SKILL

Cookie Dough Fudge

You know how fun it is to eat raw cookie dough when prepping a batch for the oven? Enter: this fudge.

INGREDIENTS

Cooking spray

¾ cup (150 grams) granulated sugar

½ cup (1 stick) unsalted butter, softened

1 teaspoon pure vanilla extract

1 cup (120 grams) all-purpose flour

1 teaspoon kosher salt

1¼ cups mini chocolate chips, divided

1 (14-ounce) can sweetened condensed milk

12 ounces white chocolate, melted (about 1½ cups)

DIRECTIONS

1 Grease an 8- or 9-inch square pan with cooking spray. Line with parchment, leaving an overhang on 2 opposite sides. In a large bowl, using a handheld mixer on medium-high speed, beat sugar, butter, and vanilla until smooth.

2 In a small microwave-save bowl, microwave flour until hot, about 1 minute.

3 Add flour and salt to butter mixture and beat until combined. Stir in 1 cup chips.

4 In a medium bowl, mix milk and white chocolate, then fold into butter mixture. Pour into prepared pan. Top with remaining ¼ cup chips. Refrigerate fudge until firm, about 2 hours.

6 Using parchment overhang, transfer fudge to a cutting board and cut into squares.

WHY DO I NEED TO HEAT THE FLOUR?

While some experts say it's okay to eat raw flour (as long as it hasn't been affected by recalls), the FDA warns against it. Some suggest heat-treating the flour by cooking it in the microwave or oven to kill off any bacteria before using it in any no-bake treat.

SKILL

FOLDING

To combine two substances with different textures (like whipped egg whites and a thicker batter, for instance), you need to stir them together with a special, gentle motion to keep the air bubbles of the lighter substance from breaking.

1
Prepare bowl. Place the heavier ingredient or mixture in a large bowl.

2
Add ingredients. Spoon about half of the lighter mixture into the bowl.

3
Scrape. Move your spatula along the bottom of the bowl out to the edge.

4–5
Fold together. Use a rubber spatula to cut through the center of the mixture down to the bottom of the bowl. Continue scraping up the side of the bowl and gently scoop the mixture over top.

6
Rotate. Turn the bowl about 90 degrees and repeat this folding motion until the mixture is combined.

7–9
Repeat. Add the second half of the lighter mixture and repeat steps 1–6 until well combined.

DON'T OVERDO IT
Don't rush, but try to use as few strokes as possible to get the job done.

WHAT YOU'LL NEED

- 2 large mixing bowls
- Measuring spoons and cups
- Whisk
- Medium mixing bowl
- Rubber spatula
- Handheld electric mixer
- Waffle iron
- Pastry brush
- Plates

TOTAL TIME
20 MINUTES

SERVES 6 TO 8

USE YOUR SKILL

Belgian Waffles

These waffles are light and fluffy on the inside and perfectly crisp on the outside. Pass the maple syrup and butter please!

INGREDIENTS

- 2 cups (240 grams) all-purpose flour
- 1 tablespoon granulated sugar
- 1 teaspoon baking powder
- ½ teaspoon baking soda
- ½ teaspoon kosher salt
- 1 cup milk
- 1 cup sour cream
- 6 tablespoons unsalted butter, melted, plus more for waffle iron and serving
- 3 large eggs, separated

  Pure maple syrup, for serving

DIRECTIONS

1. In a large bowl, whisk flour, sugar, baking powder, baking soda, and salt. In a medium bowl, whisk milk, sour cream, butter, and egg yolks. Gently fold milk mixture into dry ingredients.

2. In another large bowl, using a handheld mixer on medium-high speed, beat egg whites until stiff peaks form. Fold whipped egg whites into batter, being careful not to overmix. (A few fluffy streaks of whites are fine!)

3. Heat waffle iron according to manufacturer's instructions. Brush grates with melted butter. Spoon about ⅓ cup batter into waffle maker and cook until golden, about 5 minutes. Repeat with remaining batter.

4. Divide waffles among plates. Top with syrup and butter.

HOW DO YOU SEPARATE EGGS?

Place two small bowls on your counter. Crack an egg into one of the bowls and discard the shell. Use your fingers to gently scoop under the yellow yolk, letting the egg white drip back down into the bowl, and transfer the yolk only to the second bowl.

WHAT YOU'LL NEED

- ○ Large mixing bowl
- ○ Measuring cups
- ○ Handheld electric mixer
- ○ Rubber spatula
- ○ Spoon
- ○ Loaf pan
- ○ Serving bowls

TOTAL TIME
10 MINUTES, PLUS FREEZING TIME

SERVES 10

Cookie Butter No-Churn Ice Cream

There's no special equipment needed for this ice cream.
Just whip and fold your way to a creamy, tasty, frozen dessert.
If you want to enjoy this treat on the same day, prep it
in the morning since it will take at least four hours to freeze.

INGREDIENTS

- 3 cups heavy whipping cream
- 1 (14-ounce) can sweetened condensed milk
- ¼ cup cookie butter, such as Biscoff
- 2 cups crumbled Biscoff cookies, divided

DIRECTIONS

1. In a large bowl, using a handheld mixer on medium-high speed, beat cream and milk until stiff peaks form, about 3 minutes.

2. Slowly fold in cookie butter until well combined. Sprinkle 1 cup crumbled cookies over cream mixture and fold until incorporated.

3. Spoon mixture into a 9-inch-by-5-inch loaf pan and freeze until set, at least 4 hours or up to overnight.

4. Divide ice cream among bowls. Top with remaining 1 cup crumbled cookies.

WHAT IS BISCOFF?

Lotus Biscoff cookies, invented by a Belgian company in 1932, are crisp, rectangular shortbread cookies with a caramel and warm spice flavor.

SKILL
WHIPPING

Incorporating air into something like heavy cream to turn it from a liquid to a thick fluffy substance is called "whipping." You can whip with a stand mixer, handheld electric mixer, or simply a whisk (and some muscle!).

HOW TO WHIP WITH A WHISK

1

Prepare bowl. Place ingredient(s) in a large mixing bowl.

2–4
Whisk. With your whisk touching the bottom of the bowl, make quick, forceful side-to-side movements over and over again until you achieve the whipped consistency specified in your recipe.

HOW TO WHIP WITH A STAND OR HANDHELD MIXER

1
Prepare mixing bowl. Place ingredient(s) in the bowl of a stand mixer fitted with a whisk attachment or a large bowl if using a handheld mixer.

2
Whisk. Turn the mixer on medium–low speed and mix until foamy, about 30 seconds.

3
Whip. Increase speed to high and whip until you achieve the whipped consistency specified in your recipe.

3

2

4

WHIP IT GOOD

You're in control! Know the stages of whipped peaks and stop when you get to the right place for your recipe.

SOFT PEAKS

Cream is thick enough to hold its shape but quickly sinks back into the mixture.

MEDIUM PEAKS

Cream will hold shape and form a soft curl at the tip.

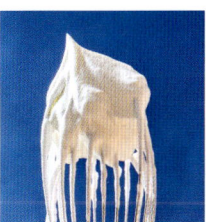

STIFF PEAKS

Cream holds its shape with a pointy tip that does not curl.

WHAT YOU'LL NEED

- Large heat-proof bowl

- Measuring spoons and cups

- Medium saucepan

- Large spatula

- Medium bowl

- Handheld mixer or whisk

- 6 ramekins or cups

- Vegetable peeler

TOTAL TIME
1 HOUR

SERVES 6

Chocolate Mousse

This fancy chocolate treat is a crowd-pleaser.
Unlike the classic French dessert, this chocolate mousse is
eggless and comes together quickly in just one hour!

INGREDIENTS

- 4 ounces chocolate or chocolate chips (semisweet, bittersweet, and/or milk chocolate), finely chopped, plus more for serving
- 1 tablespoon unsalted butter
- 1 tablespoon unsweetened cocoa powder
- ¼ teaspoon kosher salt
- 2 cups heavy cream, divided

DIRECTIONS

1 Place chocolate in a large heatproof bowl. In a medium saucepan over low heat, cook butter and cocoa powder, stirring constantly, until butter is melted and smooth. Add salt and ½ cup cream. Increase heat to medium-high and bring to a simmer. Immediately pour cream mixture over chocolate and let sit, undisturbed, until mostly melted, about 5 minutes. (Make sure chocolate is submerged in cream, but do not stir; gently tilt bowl if necessary to redistribute it.)

2 Meanwhile, in a medium bowl, using a handheld mixer on medium-high speed or a whisk, beat remaining 1½ cups cream until soft peaks form. Refrigerate until ready to use.

3 Using handheld mixer on medium-low speed or whisk, start drawing a small circle in center of chocolate mixture until just beginning to thicken and a dark, smooth vortex forms. Continue to beat in widening circles until mixture emulsifies into a uniformly thick and glossy ganache. Let sit at room temperature until no longer warm to the touch, about 5 minutes.

4 Set aside about ½ cup whipped cream for serving; refrigerate until ready to use. Using a large spatula, fold one-third of chocolate ganache into remaining whipped cream until combined. Add remaining chocolate ganache and continue to fold until no streaks remain.

5 Divide mousse among 6 ramekins or cups and refrigerate until set, about 40 minutes.

6 Top with reserved whipped cream and more chips or shaved chocolate.

HOW TO MAKE CHOCOLATE SHAVINGS
Use a vegetable peeler to shave shards off a block or bar of chocolate.

WHAT YOU'LL NEED

- 2 large mixing bowls
- Measuring spoons and cups
- Whisk
- Medium mixing bowl
- Rubber spatula
- 8-inch springform pan
- Handheld electric mixer or stand mixer with whisk attachment
- Butter knife
- Plastic wrap

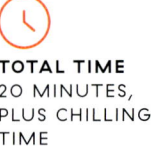

TOTAL TIME 20 MINUTES, PLUS CHILLING TIME

SERVES 8

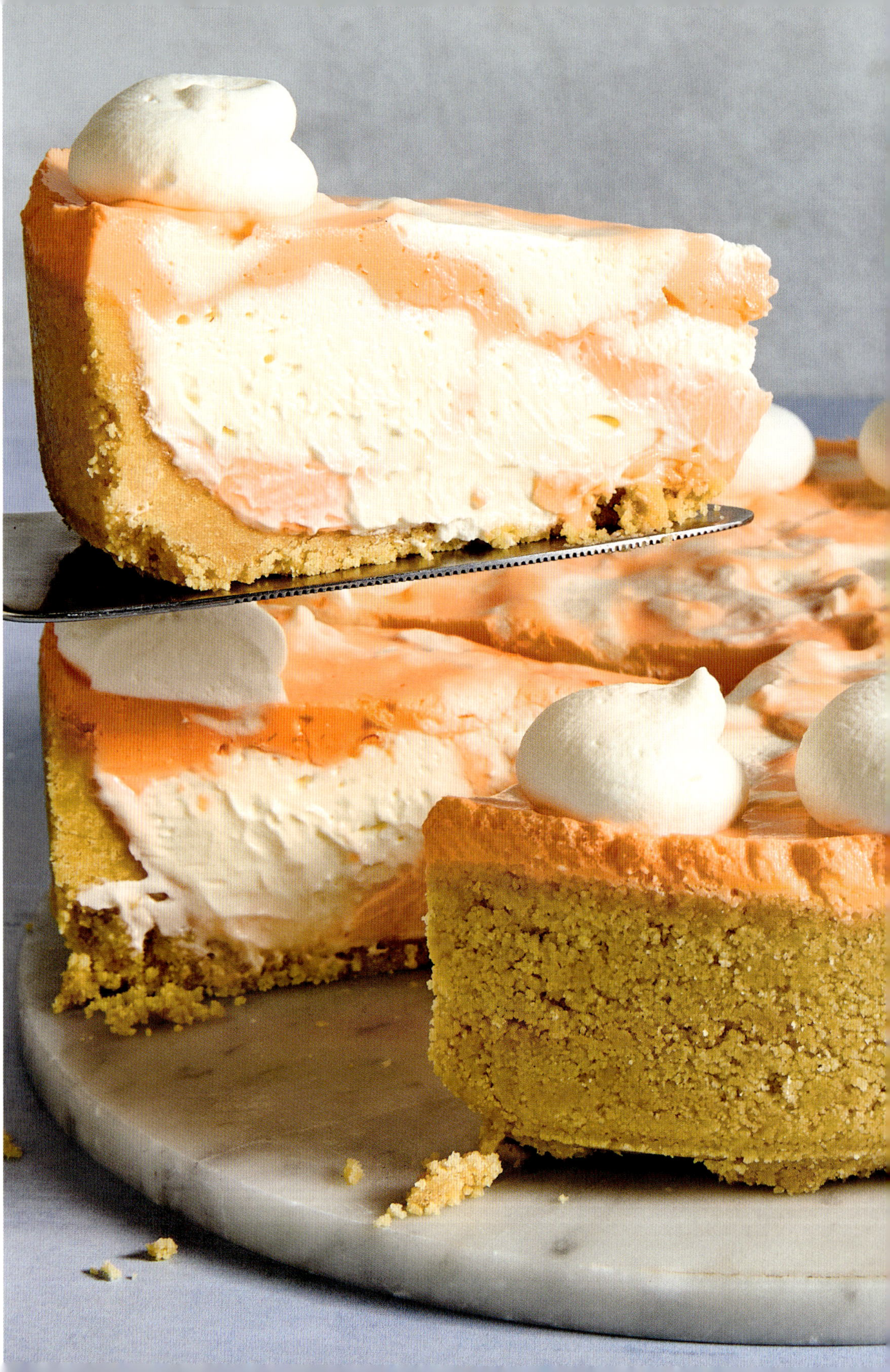

USE YOUR SKILL

Creamsicle Cheesecake

The batter might feel kind of loose as you're adding it to the pan but after a couple hours in the refrigerator, the creamy, dreamy ice-cream-treat-inspired cheesecake will be perfectly firm.

INGREDIENTS

1 cup boiling water

1 (3-ounce) box orange Jell-O

24 whole Golden Oreo cookies, crushed

6 tablespoons unsalted butter, melted

Kosher salt

2 (8-ounce) blocks cream cheese, softened

¼ cup sour cream

1 cup (115 grams) confectioners' sugar

1 teaspoon pure vanilla extract

3 cups whipped topping, divided

DIRECTIONS

1 In a large heatproof bowl, whisk boiling water and Jell-O until Jell-O is completely dissolved. Let cool.

2 In a medium bowl, mix Oreo crumbs, butter, and a pinch of salt. Press into bottom and up the sides of an 8-inch springform pan.

3 In another large bowl, using a handheld mixer or stand mixer on medium-high speed, beat cream cheese and sour cream until smooth, about 3 minutes. Add confectioners' sugar, vanilla, and a pinch of salt and beat until combined. Fold 2 cups whipped topping into cream cheese mixture, then pour half of mixture into cooled Jell-O. Whisk until smooth.

4 Onto the crust, alternate pouring ¼-cup dollops of cream cheese and Jell-O mixtures until both mixtures are used up. Using a butter knife, gently swirl the layers. Cover and refrigerate until firm, about 6 hours.

5 When firm, spoon dollops of remaining 1 cup whipped topping around outside of cheesecake.

PIPING

The next time you want to add detailed decorations on a cake or cupcake or you need precise placement of an element in a deviled egg recipe, you will be ready.

1
Prepare piping bag. Insert a piping tip (or nozzle) into a piping bag, then snip the bottom corner of the bag and push the tip through until it is snugly set.

2
Make a cuff. Fold about 3 inches of the top of the bag down to form a cuff.

3
Fill bag. Use a rubber spatula to transfer the mixture you want to pipe into the piping bag.

4
Twist bag. Unfold the cuff and twist it tightly so it both closes the bag and exerts some pressure on the mixture inside the bag.

5
Squeeze. Hold the bag between your thumb and other fingers at the twisted top and use your other hand to steady and guide the bag at the tip. Gently squeeze the bag and from the top twist to push the filling out the tip.

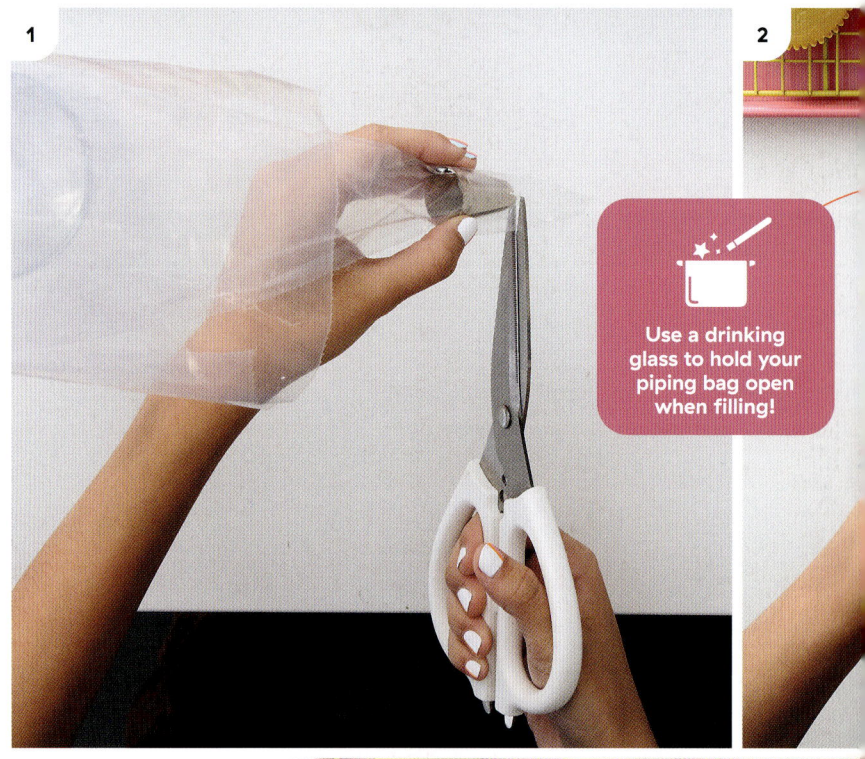

1

2

Use a drinking glass to hold your piping bag open when filling!

4

3

5

WHAT YOU'LL NEED

- Measuring spoons and cups
- Stand mixer with whisk attachment
- Large piping bag
- Large piping tip
- Small paint brush
- Drinking glass
- Rubber spatula
- 2 large baking sheets
- Parchment paper
- Ruler
- Small microwave-safe bowl

TOTAL TIME
4 HOURS AND 30 MINUTES, PLUS COOLING TIME

MAKES 35 TO 40

Peppermint Meringues

Minty, chocolate–dipped meringues are an impressive addition to any holiday dessert table. Just make sure to really let them rest in the oven after they're done baking to prevent cracks.

INGREDIENTS

- 4 large egg whites
- ¼ teaspoon cream of tartar
- ¼ teaspoon kosher salt
- 1 cup (200 grams) granulated sugar
- ½ teaspoon peppermint extract

  Red gel food coloring
- 1 cup semisweet chocolate chips
- 5 small peppermint canes or candies, crushed

DIRECTIONS

1 Preheat oven to 200°F.

2 In the large bowl of a stand mixer fitted with the whisk attachment, beat egg whites, cream of tartar, and salt on medium speed until whites are foamy and soft peaks form, about 1 minute. With mixer running, slowly add sugar 1 tablespoon at a time, then increase speed to high and beat until meringue is thick, marshmallow–like, and holds firm peaks, 4 to 6 minutes. Beat in peppermint extract.

3 Fit a large piping bag with a large tip and fold top back to create a cuff. Using a small paint brush, paint a few thin vertical stripes of red food coloring inside bag. Rest bag in an empty drinking glass to prop it up, then use a rubber spatula to scrape meringue into piping bag. Fold back top of bag and twist top to seal.

4 Pipe 2–inch rounds on 2 large parchment–lined baking sheets, spacing 1 inch apart. Bake until cookies are very crisp and hard to the touch, 1½ to 2 hours. Turn off oven and let cookies sit in oven until completely cool, about 2 hours.

5 In a small microwave–safe bowl, microwave chocolate chips in 30–second intervals, stirring between each, until melted and smooth.

6 Working with one cookie at a time, dip bottom of meringue in chocolate and let excess drip off. Sprinkle some crushed peppermints over chocolate and return immediately to baking sheet. Repeat with remaining cookies, then refrigerate until chocolate is set, 15 to 20 minutes.

WHAT YOU'LL NEED

- 9-inch springform pan or cake pan
- Parchment paper
- Measuring spoons and cups
- Chef's knife
- Cutting board
- Small mixing bowl
- Medium mixing bowl
- Whisk
- Large mixing bowl
- Handheld mixer
- Zip-top bags
- Rubber spatula
- Oven mitts
- Wire rack
- Cake stand or platter
- Large piping bag
- Large star tip

TOTAL TIME
1 HOUR

SERVES 8 TO 12

Oreo Cookie Cake

There are desserts that spark pure joy, and this oversized cookie cake is one of them. It's giving Oreo everything with the sandwich cookie mixed into the batter, buttercream, and also used to decorate.

INGREDIENTS

FOR THE COOKIE CAKE

Cooking spray

12   Oreo cookies

2   cups (240 grams) plus 2 tablespoons all-purpose flour

1½   teaspoons kosher salt

1   teaspoon baking soda

¾   cup (1½ sticks) unsalted butter, melted, slightly cooled

¾   cup (160 grams) packed light brown sugar

⅓   cup (67 grams) granulated sugar

1   large egg

1   large egg yolk

1   tablespoon pure vanilla extract

FOR THE BUTTERCREAM & ASSEMBLY

11   Oreo cookies, divided

½   cup (1 stick) unsalted butter, room temperature

2   tablespoons (or more) whole milk or cream

2   tablespoons unsweetened cocoa powder

½   teaspoon pure vanilla extract

1½   cups (175 grams) (or more) confectioners' sugar

DIRECTIONS

1 **Make the cookie cake** Place a rack in center of oven; preheat to 350°F. Grease a 9-inch springform pan or cake pan with cooking spray. Line bottom of pan with parchment, then grease parchment with cooking spray.

2 Coarsely chop each Oreo (6 to 8 pieces per cookie) and transfer to a small bowl. (Don't include the fine crumbs that fall off when chopping; either discard or reserve for the Oreo buttercream frosting.) In a medium bowl, whisk flour, salt, and baking soda until combined.

3 In a large bowl, using a handheld mixer on medium-high speed, beat butter, brown sugar, and granulated sugar until smooth and fluffy. Add egg, egg yolk, and vanilla and beat, scraping down bowl as needed, until well incorporated. Add dry ingredients and beat on low speed until just combined.

4 Using a spatula, fold in Oreos (you don't want to crush them with the mixer); reserve a few pieces for the top. Spread dough into prepared pan, then press reserved pieces on top.

5 Bake cake until lightly golden across the top and just firm to the touch, 20 to 24 minutes (it'll continue to firm up as it cools). Transfer pan to a wire rack and let cool.

6 **Make the buttercream** Place 5 Oreos in a zip-top bag, seal, and crush with a rolling pin until fine crumbs form.

7 In a large bowl, using handheld mixer on medium-high speed, beat butter until smooth. Add crushed Oreos, milk, cocoa powder, and vanilla and beat on medium speed, scraping down bowl as needed, until well combined, about 2 minutes. Reduce mixer speed to low. Gradually add confectioners' sugar, a little at a time, and beat, scraping down bowl as needed, until incorporated. Increase mixer speed to high and continue to beat until fluffy, about 1 minute more. Add more milk or confectioners' sugar until desired consistency is reached.

8 Remove cake from pan; discard parchment. Place cake on a cake stand or platter. Pipe Oreo buttercream in decorative mounds around the perimeter. Cut remaining 6 Oreos in half. Nestle halved Oreos around the perimeter.

INDEX + CREDITS

Index

W

X

Y

Z

Credits

Photographs by Lucy Schaeffer

Food styling by Taylor Ann Spencer, Francesca Zani and Makinze Gore

Props courtesy Williams Sonoma

Manicures by Miss Pop Nails

Thank you to the 13 kids who came to the Delish kitchens to perfect these culinary skills. We hope you used your new skills while cooking at home with your families.

Recipe Photography

Erik Bernstein: 28, 70, 74, 114, 118, 184

Rachel Vanni: 30, 50, 54, 62, 100, 112, 120, 146, 152

Lucy Schaeffer: 34, 40, 80, 88, 106, 108, 158

Bryan Gardner: 36

Julia Gartland: 42, 48, 64, 76, 96, 134, 154, 172, 178

Rocky Luten: 56, 102, 144, 176

Nico Schinco: 68, 69, 160

Ryan Liebe: 82, 83, 126

Andrew Bui: 85, 109, 128, 164

Doaa Elkady: 86

Parker Feierbach: 94, 138, 166, 170

Kate Jordan: 132

Joseph De Leo: 140

Dane Tashima: 182

Recipe Developers

Lena Abraham: 29, 41, 51, 69, 107, 165, 167, 179

Lindsay Funston: 31, 109

Laura Rege: 35, 49, 77, 97, 127, 135, 161

Gabriella Stern: 37, 83

Taylor Ann Spencer: 43, 63, 71, 87

Makinze Gore: 55, 81, 95, 101, 113, 115, 139, 153, 159

Bethany Morrison: 57, 65

Francesca Zani: 75, 129, 141

Lauren Miyashiro: 103, 145, 147, 171

Emily Connor: 119, 185

Gabby Romero: 121

Alejandro Valdes Lora: 133

Candace Braun Davison: 155

Joanna Saltz: 173

Adrienne Anderson: 177

Olivia Mack Maccool: 183

Recipe Food Stylists

Makinze Gore: 28, 36, 74, 80, 128, 144, 172, 176, 178, 184

Barrett Washburne: 30

Taylor Ann Spencer: 34, 56, 108

Lena Abraham: 40, 62

Adrienne Anderson: 42, 48, 64, 76, 96, 112, 126, 134, 146, 152, 154

Brooke Caison: 50, 54, 68, 69, 82, 83, 86, 100, 102, 106, 118, 120, 132, 140, 160

Simon Andrews: 70

Spencer Richards: 114

Jason Schreiber: 182

Stock photography

Getty Images 29, 63, 65, 67

Illustration

ROCIO EGIO: back cover, inside front cover

Icons

The Noun Project (front cover, 4, 5, 9, 25, 32, 35, 38, 39, 41, 51, 53, 60, 71, 73, 81, 92, 95, 103, 105, 113, 124, 125, 133, 136, 142, 143, 145, 151, 157, 162, 163, 174, 175)

Acknowledgements

It might be my name as the author on the cover, but there wouldn't even be a book without all the amazing minds who create and contribute to it. I'm so deeply grateful for their dedication to the Delish brand and their commitment to always making our content the best and most fun in the whole world. But I'm especially proud of the way the team works so hard to include all levels and ages of cooks—because everyone deserves a little something Delish. —*Joanna Saltz*

DELISH

Editorial Director: Joanna Saltz

Executive Content Editor: Carissa Tozzi

Creative Director: Jessica Musumeci

Senior Director, Content Operations: Lindsey Ramsey

Senior Food Director: Robert Seixas

Director Of Community & Audience Development: Julia Smith

Visual Director: Rebecca Simpson Steele

Deputy Recipe Editor: Jill Baughman

Senior Food Editor: Makinze Gore

Food Editor: Brooke Caison

Assistant Food Editors: Taylor Ann Spencer, Francesca Zani

Editorial Business Manager: Megan Belair

Visual Production Coordinators: Temira Greene, Cindy Roblero

Test Kitchen Manager: Alejandro Valdes Lora

HEARST HOME KIDS

Vice President, Publisher, Hearst Books: Jacqueline Deval

Deputy Director, Hearst Books: Nicole Fisher

Creative Director, Hearst Product Studio: Gillian MacLeod

Book Designer: Alyce Jones

Book Writer: Katie Leaird

Deputy Managing Editor, Hearst Books: Maria Ramroop

Senior Sales & Marketing Coordinator: Nicole Plonski

PUBLISHED BY HEARST

President & Chief Executive Officer: Steven R. Swartz

Chairman: William R. Hearst III

Executive Vice Chairman: Frank A. Bennack, Jr.

HEARST MAGAZINE MEDIA, INC.

President: Debi Chirichella

General Manager, Hearst Lifestyle Group: Ronak Patel

Global Chief Revenue Officer: Lisa Ryan Howard

Editorial Director: Lucy Kaylin

Chief Financial & Strategy Officer: Regina Buckley

Consumer Growth Officer: Lindsey Horrigan

Chief Product & Technology Officer: Daniel Bernard

President, Hearst Magazines International: Jonathan Wright

Secretary: Catherine A. Bostron

Publishing Consultants: Gilbert C. Maurer, Mark F. Miller

Library of Congress Cataloging-in-Publication Data Available on Request

10 9 8 7 6 5 4 3 2 1

Published by Hearst Home Kids, an imprint of Hearst Books/Hearst Magazine Media, Inc.
300 W 57th Street
New York, NY 10019

Delish, Hearst Home Kids, the Hearst Home Kids logo, and Hearst Books are registered trademarks of Hearst Communications, Inc.

For information about custom editions, special sales, premium and corporate purchases: hearst.com/magazines/hearst-books

Printed in China
978-1-958395-73-8